CRAP LYRICS

I'd like to dedicate this book to the thousands of songwriters over the years who have sweated blood in the pursuit of songwriting excellence, the men and women who have stood before the lord of song with nothing on their tongue but 'Hallelujah'. Or something not quite that good.

I hope you'll forgive me my mockery. It's only because I'm jealous. And a failed musician, obviously. Mind you, I'm not that failed – have you seen my song on the internet? Not too bad, is it? If you think I've got promise, don't hesitate to get in touch at craplyrics@googlemail.com

First published in the United Kingdom in 2009 by
Portico Books
10 Southcombe Street
London
W14 0RA

An imprint of Anova Books Company Ltd

ISBN 9781906032593

A CIP catalogue record for this book is available from the British Library.

10 9 8 7 6 5 4 3

Typeset by SX Composing DTP, Rayleigh, Essex
Printed and bound by WS Bookwell, Finland

This book can be ordered direct from the publisher at www.anovabooks.com

JOHNNY SHARP

CRAP LYRICS

a celebration of the very worst
pop lyrics of all time... EVER!

PORTICO

CONTENTS

INTRODUCTION

'Words,' said the 1983 one-hit wonder F R David in his song of the same name, 'don't come easy.' That must have been particularly true for Mr David in this instance, since he was a French–Tunisian musician for whom English was not a native tongue. Yet his admission struck a chord, not just among tongue-tied lovers around the world, but among struggling songwriters grappling with the slippery task of adding words to their music.

Many performers have said, 'My songs are like my children'. If so, there are some seriously neglected kids running around, and it's invariably the lyrical side of their development that hasn't been shown due care and attention. At the very least, the musical wing of the NSPCC might want to step in, and offer some stern advice on parenting skills. After all, many songwriters don't even bother thinking about their offspring's names, sex, personality, hair colour or how many toes they have until they're lacing up their shoes on the first day of school.

That's partly because lyrics are often the last thing musicians consider before they record a song. Being a feckless, pampered and workshy breed at the best of times, they will put off the daunting job of setting their thoughts to music until the last possible moment, when one of them – usually the singer, if it's a band – will spend a few quiet minutes in the studio toilets scanning the graffiti for inspiration and frantically scribbling down lines as the glockenspiel parts are being recorded.

Bearing that in mind, what is surprising is not that there are so many bad lyrics out there, but that there are so few.

I get the odd night when I'm halfway through 'Don't Look Back In Anger' when I say to myself, 'I still don't know what these words mean! I'm thinking, what the . . . what the . . . 'Stand up beside the fireplace'. Why?

And all these kids will be singing it at the top of their voices with all their arms around each other and I kind of feel like stopping and going, 'Look, can somebody help me out here? Am I missing something?'

Noel Gallagher, *The Observer,* **2005**

Of course, many songwriters would probably tell you that lyrics are a relatively unimportant part of a song, and that they don't have to convey any specific meaning or resonance to the listener, merely a vague 'feel' that seems to fit the vibe of the music. And sometimes that's true. A song can work brilliantly despite bad lyrics (may I direct you to exhibit A from Chapter 2, Oasis's 'Champagne Supernova'?). But it rarely works because of them.

At their best, lyrics give a song a large part of its identity, and strike as much of a chord in the listener as the saddest of D minors. Would 'Yesterday' be half the song it is if Paul McCartney had stuck with his first-draft opening line of 'Scrambled eggs, oh my darling how I love your legs'?

Yet the vast majority of popular song lyrics manage to pass in and out of our ears without arousing too much attention. This book is mostly dedicated to the small minority of lyrics that simply leap out of the speakers and make normally tolerant music lovers wince as if they'd just caught a whiff of Amy Winehouse's breath.

Magazines and newspapers regularly furnish us with long lists of 'albums to hear before you die'. I'd argue that some of the words in this book are 'lyrics to die before you hear'.

Sadly, it's probably too late for that. In all likelihood you'll have come across most of them at some point, and while you will recognise some and agree that they represent an unacceptable stain on our great language, others may be excerpts from your favourite songs. Indeed someone, somewhere, probably has the words of Steve Miller's 'The Joker' tattooed on their neck, and believes that they too are a space cowboy, and a 'pompatus of love'.

You may, of course, ask if it's strictly fair that we are pointing and laughing at the hard work of talented musicians, holding it up to the scorn of the world? Well, that's debatable. And the answer to that debate is 'yes'.

As much great pop has been inspired by negative feelings as positive ones, and just as we demand passion from performers, they demand it from listeners in return, so they can't expect us to be passive, uncritical consumers.

If my mum was one of the songwriters criticised in this book, she would undoubtedly ask 'Well, could you do any better'? I can't categorically confirm that I could, although at certain points I have attempted to do worse. See what you think.

Either way, I'm not claiming to be any major literary authority. And like the songwriters whose work I so cheaply mock, I'm bound to make clumsy and contradictory statements, and while I hope I can avoid cliché, I'm not about to lose sleep over it.

You also shouldn't think that I'm condemning all the records in which these words are found. A lyric of debatable quality is no major obstacle to a great song – in fact, sometimes it even enhances its charm. I have an enduring affection for many of the songs featured here, and many other readers will love them too. And someone, somewhere, must love 'The Cheeky Song'. Mustn't they?

A bad lyric is rarely the sign of a bad artist. Many of the artists featured in this book are actually among the greatest lyricists in the history of popular music – the likes of Dylan, Weller or Barlow. OK, maybe scratch that last one. Many of the lyrics here would have gone unnoticed if they hadn't been included in very popular and often otherwise well-crafted compositions. Some of them sound very fine indeed when heard coming out of a radio, even if they look pretty dumb on paper.

Inevitably, a bad lyric is in the ear of the beholder. One person's nonsensical drivel is another's inspired impression-istic genius. Besides, it's far from necessary to make any conventional sense whatsoever to impart meaning in this game. When Little Richard sang 'Awopbopaloobopawop bamboom' he was hardly trying to impress anyone with his mastery of the English language, but as a gleeful, unhinged expression of joy it's one of the most incendiary utterances ever recorded.

However, none of these mitigating points are going to stop me taking great musicians' words completely out of context, then pointing and laughing at them as if they were David

Cameron attempting to impress a group of inner-city children by doing an 'olly' on his skateboard.

Ultimately, I come not to simply bury bad lyrics, but to dig them up, like a dog returning to sniff its own waste with a mixture of affection and horrified fascination. If I may conclude in the style to which you will shortly become accustomed . . .

I hope you enjoy these lyrical examples
Please send me some of your own favourite samples
email me at: craplyrics@googlemail.com
I'll do my best to read every one
I cannot enter into personal correspondence
But I promise to read everything once
Singing 'la la la la ay ay ay ay moosey'

CHAPTER 1

SERIOUS AS CANCER

Rhymes against humanity – Part One

You could probably fill this entire book with rhymes that flow as smoothly as a dead crocodile through a U-bend, as they are by far the most common and most immediately noticeable form of lyrical clanger. But we have a whole world of wrongs to cover in these pages, so we've dedicated a mere two chapters to them.

In this the first of those chapters you will find everything from relatively forgivable 'rhymes of passion' (committed on the spur of the moment, with a certain 'will this do?' quality) to cold, calculated rhyme rampages in which the culprits could hardly have insulted our great language any further if they had dug up Shakespeare's corpse and dirty danced with it, then called his mum a slag. We might as well throw you in at the deep end, then . . .

LIFE
DES'REE

In times of crisis, songwriters will instinctively invoke primal urges, such as hunger, thirst, or a big fat KitKat wrapper full of 'brown'. How else can we explain the sentiments of this 1998 hit, wherein Des admits, **I don't want to see a ghost, it's the sight that I fear most. I'd rather eat a piece of toast, and watch the evening news**.

It is customary, when describing something you really dislike, to say 'I'd rather...' and then include something suitably horrific, such as 'drown in a vat of Karen Matthews' hair grease' or 'be stuck in a lift with Andrew Castle'. There is a slim possibility that Des'ree has a lifelong phobia of toast, and deliberately avoids walking past Currys in case she sees a Russell Hobbs Retro Four Slice at half price in the window. But my guess is that she went through the rhyme options for 'ghost', considered 'even more than a nuclear bomb in the post', and then remembered that she didn't have any breakfast that morning.

Thanks to that rush of blood from stomach to head, everyone now remembers this line more than any of her hits. There's no justice. But at least she's got some fairly esteemed company.

Don't Pass Me By
THE BEATLES

All the greats have dabbled in the murky waters of rhyminality[1]. You'll surely have heard this rollicking romp, in which Ringo foghorns, **I'm sorry that I doubted you, I was so unfair. You were in a car crash, and you lost your hair**.

When it was written in 1968, this line was taken to be further evidence for the conspiracy theory that Paul McCartney had died in a car crash some months earlier. Thankfully for him, it was merely evidence of what happens when you let the drummer write songs.

[1] I will occasionally refer to lyrical wrongdoers as 'rhyminals'. I realise this is wordplay worthy of Richard Stilgoe after one too many Bristol Creams, but like many of the artists featured in this chapter, I don't care. It'll do, I've got a book to write, and you try looking for alternative words for 'rhyme', let alone puns involving it. Never apologise, never explain. Although I think I just did.

Roller Skating Child
THE BEACH BOYS

The Beatles' esteemed contemporaries dropped a similar stinker here, albeit in 1977, by which time Brian Wilson was ankle deep in his sand–pit barking at the moon and no one was really listening to their new songs. **I go and get my skates on and I catch up with her**, they sing. **We do it holding hands, it's so cold I go 'Brrrr!'**

Ouch. Still, they should be glad they didn't end up among the sleazy denizens of Chapter 3, considering they tell of how **we'll make sweet lovin' when the sun goes down, We'll even do more when your mama's not around.**

'Hello, is that Social Services? I've just seen a group of bearded musicians loitering by a frozen lake, acting suspiciously . . .'

Highly Strung
SPANDAU BALLET

Until recently, the infamous line **She used to be a diplomat, and now she's down the laundromat** was regarded as somewhat laughable. We chuckled not only at the iffy rhyme but the faintly farcical scenario presented therein. Yet in this era of global recession, their words could prove prophetic – could we see a queue of well-travelled executives lining up for a service wash after they are forced to lay off their domestic servants and flog the tumble dryer? They also say of the former diplomat in question, 'They washed her mind'. Does that cost extra?

Rhythm Is A Dancer
SNAP

Turbo B, the rapper who fronted this Europop outfit, was probably unaware that he was uttering the words that will one day later be inscribed on his gravestone when he boomed, **I'm serious as cancer when I say rhythm is a dancer!**

He may not have written them himself, but we still have to ask the question:

JUST HOW SERIOUS CAN YOU POSSIBLY BE WHEN YOU'RE SAYING 'RHYTHM IS A DANCER'?

You can perhaps be as serious as you like when you're saying 'My house is on fire and I am currently trapped inside it', but rhythm's status as a dancer is surely unlikely to be a life-endangering situation, even if, as Inner Circle suggest later in Chapter 2, the dancer might be sweating until they can sweat no more. The only possibility that could redeem this line is that Turbo hasn't told us the full story. If, of course, he'd announced, 'I'm serious as cancer when I say Rhythm is a dancer who has just been kidnapped by radical Islamic jihad militia and is being held without food and water while chained to a radiator in a dark Islamabad cellar' then we would have fully understood the gravity of the situation.

Is There Something I Should Know?
DURAN DURAN

Simon Le Bon and co should know the danger of overstatement better than anyone after the unforgettable observation that **fiery demons all dance when you walk through that door, don't say you're easy on me, you're about as easy as a nuclear war.**

I think you'll agree, they've overcooked the comparison. A nuclear war would, there's no doubt, be far from easy. All that death and destruction, eating clumps of your own hair in an underground shelter and slowly dying from radiation sickness – what a chore. But a mildly difficult romantic partner wouldn't quite be in the same league. Whereas if he'd said, 'You're about as easy as finding an unrestricted parking spot in the centre of Colchester on market day', we couldn't really have argued.

Pink
AEROSMITH

If Steven Tyler's creaky old knees ever give up on him, there's a gap in the market for a man who can describe colours accurately and succinctly. He was the man, after all, who sang **Pink when I turn out the light. Pink – it's like red but not quite.**

Yeah, tell it like it is, Stevie! I for one would be only too happy to go into my local DIY shop and, instead of finding colour shadings that sound like euphemisms for drugs, like 'intense apple' or 'Moroccan velvet', you'd get straight-talking descriptions like 'Nearly black but got scared', 'Would have been mauve but the magenta ink cartridge was running low' or indeed 'Well on the way to yellow but stumbled at the last hurdle and got splashed with a pot of cream'.

THAT WAS THEN, THIS IS NOW
ABC

Martin Fry of ABC professed his joy at being voted into the top ten of worst ever lyrics in a BBC poll a few years back. And I think we can confirm he was worthy of the accolade thanks to this passage: **More sacrifices than an Aztec priest, Standing here straining at that leash. All fall down, can't complain, mustn't grumble – help yourself to another piece of apple crumble.**

He might try to argue that once he'd used the word 'grumble' his rhyming options were limited. But what was wrong with rumble, fumble, humble, mumble, stumble, tumble or even possibly womble? Or dumbbell?

I actually rang Martin Fry, asking for an explanation. I only got his answering machine. He said he couldn't come to the phone, as he was being kept on a leash today, making one of his regular sacrifices to the gods. He said not to worry though – he's being well fed with popular British puddings.

Buck Rogers
FEEDER

We all dream of escape from time to time, to a land of sunshine and good times, where we can leave all our cares behind and duck out of the rat race. Somewhere like . . . Exeter, perhaps?

That's what was presumably on Grant Nicholas of Feeder's mind when he wrote 'Buck Rogers', a radio-friendly pop song in which he sings, **We'll start over again, grow ourselves new skin. Get a house in Devon, drink cider from a lemon**.

Now, I know they're into New Age practices down there in the South-west, but this sounds more like some bizarre religious cult. I'm imagining allotments full of human skin, and people drinking cider from lemons, quietly muttering to each other, 'They're a bit small, as drinking receptacles go, aren't they? Why can't we just drink lemon from a lemon?'

The more smart-arsed among you might point out that human beings grow new skin all the time, so maybe we can't argue with that part of the equation. But drinking cider from a lemon? You might as well drink wine from a fax machine.

But anything goes in this brave new society, especially when Brother Grant announces he is the son of God, and he has put something special in those lemons to transport his disciples to the next world.

FIX YOU
COLDPLAY

It is traditional when considering an artist's 'work' to divide it into 'periods'. To give you some examples, Picasso's *Les Desmoiselles D'Avignon* is the most famous piece of his 'African' period, Bob Dylan's *Saved* and *Slow Train Coming* are said to come from his 'Christian' period, and Neil Young's synth rock adventure *Trans* is part of his 'titting about with a vocoder like Uncle Jeff at Christmas hitting the bossa nova button on his new Bontempi organ' period.

Likewise, this song can be seen as part of Coldplay's 'rhyming' era, wherein lyricist Chris Martin began to use couplets in much the same way an OCD sufferer uses soap. He was soon displaying a wholehearted passion for activities like wanting to be just you and me in a boat on the sea, drinking cups of tea with no great need to have a pee.

All harmless fun, for the most part. But when he promised on this hit single that **Lights will guide you home, and ignite your bones**, the collective intake of breath from radio listeners must have been sufficient to divert global weather currents.

I'm guessing that most people's initial thought would have been, 'Thanks for the thought, Chris, but I'm not sure setting light to my bones will actually do me much good in the long term.'

It's understandable that you might want to warm someone's bones with the glow of the light of your enduring love, but igniting them would surely be going way too far. Besides, last time I checked, bones didn't readily lend themselves to being set alight, unlike, say, paper or matches.

It would surely require several years' supply of Ready Brek[1] consumed in a single sitting to actually induce spontaneous combustion, combined with large amounts of a highly flammable liquid, like, say, alcohol. By which time, if he tried it, Chris Martin would probably sound more like Tom Waits singing the hits of Impaled Nazarene. Which, come to think of it, may not be such a bad idea.

[1] For those readers born outside the UK or after 1985, Ready Brek is a popular oat-based British breakfast cereal which was advertised for many years using the highly suspect suggestion that consuming it would make your child glow with warmth, as if they'd swallowed liquid plutonium. And no one even reported them to *That's Life* (2).

[2] For those readers BOTUKOA1985, *That's Life* was a popular consumer programme in which toothy harridan Esther Rantzen and a harem of turtle-necked man-slaves stuck up for the nation's consumer rights. Then Doc Cox[3] sang a 'zany' song about it.

[3] Oh, look him up on the bloody internet.

Chapter 2

Isn't It Ironic? Well, No, Not REALLY

Lyrics that just don't add up

It has been claimed that writing about music is like dancing about architecture — an exercise that makes very little sense. Yet I've managed to make a living out of it. And in case you're interested, I also on occasion do the jitterbug in tribute to Norman Foster's majestic 'gherkin' building, and indeed a slightly dejected tango as a means of expressing my disappointment at the linear shape and neo-brutalist style of the Centre Point building just off London's Oxford Street.

Likewise, the language of pop music is full of sentences and statements that are absurd and nonsensical, but like a speech by John Prescott, it's often only when we look at them written down that we realise the full extent of their abuse of common sense, scientific fact, and the natural order of things.

CHAMPAGNE SUPERNOVA
OASIS

A perfect example of a song whose words sound pretty good . . . until you actually listen to them. The protagonist of this song is, after all, **slowly walking down the hall, faster than a cannonball.** I know Oasis never made any secret of their liking for drugs, but this sounds suspiciously like the time-warping effects of Chris Morris's spoof drug 'Cake' from *Brass Eye*, which made unsuspecting pill-poppers believe they had a month to cross the road. Could being chained to the mirror and the razor blade have had an effect on Noel Gallagher's Shatner's Bassoon?

We are later assured that someday, we will find our increasingly unreliable narrator **caught beneath the landslide in a champagne supernova in the sky**. Now that image throws up so many profound questions. Do they have landslides in the sky? And where exactly is the singer, Liam Gallagher, positioned if he's beneath the landslide, but 'in' a champagne supernova?

A supernova is defined on Wikipedia as 'a stellar explosion that creates an extremely luminous object'. Just imagine an exploding, luminous Liam Gallagher in the sky. As Patrick Moore gazes through his telescope one night, he suddenly sees bits of snorkel parka, a haircut that Paul Weller gave to charity in 1994, six days' stubble and a couple of legs still stuck in the familiar baboon-shuffle position slowly floating across the stars. Then picture a champagne version of that – sticky, loud and endlessly bloody annoying. As for the position of the landslide in all this . . . well maybe it's not such a bad idea. After all, if you were stuck in space with Liam Gallagher for company, you'd want to bury him too.

BACK FOR GOOD
TAKE THAT

Picture the scene. You've had a row with your partner after some unspecified heinous crime on your part. They're clearly very angry – they've stormed out, and if this was *EastEnders*, the 'Boof! Boof! Boof!' drums that precede the end credits would undoubtedly start to sound.

So you're begging for forgiveness, but there's a problem. However carefully you compose and rehearse your speech to win them back, your own feeble, stuttering words are not strong enough to adequately convey your feelings.

Then you hit on an idea. How wonderfully romantic would it be to use a famous line from a classic pop ballad? Yes! That's got to be a winner. So, without really thinking twice, you blurt it out.

'The thing is, darling . . . **whatever I said, whatever I did, I didn't mean it. I just want you back for good**.'

If it was my girlfriend, I think I can have an educated guess at the likely response.

Girlfriend: *You what?!* You . . . Oh. My. God. You are incredible. Unbelievable. *(Insert look of contempt normally seen on the mother of a murdered teenager staring across the dock at the accused)*

HOW CAN YOU SAY YOU DIDN'T MEAN IT IF YOU DON'T EVEN KNOW WHAT YOU DID, AND YOU DON'T EVEN KNOW WHAT YOU SAID?!

Me: Erm . . . yeah, fair point. Look, anyway, I've brought you some flowers.

Girlfriend: Yeah? Well, you know where you can stick them. And don't you ever, *ever* quote Take That lyrics to me again. I was always an East Seventeeny. (Storms out)

HORSE WITH NO NAME
AMERICA

Musically, this Anglo-American trio's 1971 chart-topper is a thing of rare beauty, with wonderfully trippy folk-rock harmonies married to a lazy, clip-clopping tempo. Yet the only excuse they could possibly make for the accompanying words is that they were still suffering the effects of the brown acid at Woodstock[1].

The first of many questionable claims is the narrator's central statement that he has **been through the desert on a horse with no name, it felt good to be out of the rain**. While many of us would step indoors to get out of the rain, he has somehow managed to find himself in a desert, on a horse with no name, one which presumably has many camel-like qualities to stop it dying of thirst.

He then observes, **in the desert, you can remember your name, for there ain't no one for to give you no pain**. That's got to be the first and last time that anyone has suggested that several days' horse ride through a desert could serve as a cure for amnesia. But if he's feeling that inspired, couldn't he have got round to naming the horse? Even if he just decided to start calling it 'Dobbin', I doubt anyone would be running across the sand waving its birth certificate to tell him otherwise.

Among other curious phenomena the singer reports is the startling revelation that **the heat was hot**.

The plot thickens when he sings, **After two days in the desert sun, my skin began to turn red**. Which begs the question – just how 'hot' was this 'heat', and where exactly was this desert? On the outskirts of Glasgow? Somewhere in central Finland? After all, you'd have thought even the most modest desert sun would have rosed him up a treat long before the 48-hour mark, especially back in 1971 when this song was written, a time when 'sunblock' meant a knotted hanky on your head. Perhaps the desert was actually somewhere off the M25, since although the band is called America, this song was written by their British singer Dewey Bunnell, a man with little or no knowledge of deserts. He later admitted he had written the song as something of a fantasy as he sat in his London flat staring out at the rain.

But we digress. He continues the story, relating how **after nine days, I let the horse run free 'cos the desert had turned to sea. There were plants and birds and rocks and things** ...

And 'things'? What things? Come on, you can do better than that, surely? And hang on – plants and birds and rocks? And as for the horse, how could the poor nag run anywhere after nine days in the desert? So many questions. Then we are informed that **the ocean is a desert with its life underground**

and the perfect disguise above.

OK, so the ocean is a desert, except for the major defining feature of a desert, which is an almost total lack of water, or fish.

What a fertile imagination Mr Bunnell has, quite apart from believing he's from America. But we should perhaps point out at this point that the word 'horse' is a popular slang name for heroin.

It just goes to reinforce a couple of well-known nuggets of advice: Namely, 'Write about what you know', and 'Just say no, kids'.

[1] At some point at the legendary free hippy festival, an announcement was made from the stage to warn people against taking 'the brown acid' that was circulating, since there were reports of some users experiencing bad trips from it. Whereas any other tab of unspecified substance bought from a shifty-looking black marketeer who you didn't know from Charles Manson was bound to be perfectly safe, right?

MacArthur Park
RICHARD HARRIS / DONNA SUMMER ET AL

In any realm of the written word, extending metaphors is a perilous business. Like running with scissors, it's always likely to end in tears and possible injury, if not to the person then certainly to the reputation.

So it proved in the memorable chorus of this lachrymose 1968 lament, written by the usually peerless Jimmy Webb and popularised by Richard Harris and later Donna Summer. It begins with the abstruse observation that **someone left the cake out in the rain**. They sound particularly devastated about the demise of this cake, perhaps more devastated than any sane human being should ever get about a cake. In fact, they admit that **I don't think that I can take it, 'cos it took so long to bake it, and I'll never have that recipe again! Oh no!**

I'm assuming they're actually referring, however obliquely, to a relationship. But maybe it's just me. Maybe you can easily visualise this common scenario. You've baked a cake, hoping to seduce that special someone with it. You've given it to this mysterious 'someone' to look after, though God knows why if you care about it that much. Maybe they've promised to put some extra-special icing on it, and were just bringing it back when they got distracted by a rare butterfly fluttering through the area, left the cake on a bench, then realised they'd left their hair-straighteners on, and dashed straight back home, completely forgetting about the cake. Then wouldn't you just know it, it bloomin' well goes and rains!

It wouldn't be such a disaster, but the recipe, written on a piece of paper, was also sticking out of it, and the rain made all the ink run, so it's now illegible. And you can never get another recipe because . . . well, maybe it was given to you by someone who is now dead, or by a stranger who then left without leaving even so much as a name to look up on Facebook. And while you may make other cakes in the future, you'll never be able to bake one with the seductive powers that one had.

It's so easy to think it'll never happen to you.

FANTASY SONG TITLES TOP TEN: CAKE

1. BROWN GIRL IN THE MERINGUE
2. UNBREAK MY TART
3. TAKE ME DANCING CAKE-ED IN THE RAIN
4. I WANT TO CAKE UP WITH YOU
5. RUNAROUND SOUFFLE
6. THANK YOU FOR SENDING ME AN ANGEL CAKE
7. LIFE ON MARZIPAN
8. SWISS ROLL WITH IT
9. FEAR OF A BLACK FOREST GATEAU PLANET
10. STOP KICKING MY TART AROUND

MISSING
EVERYTHING BUT THE GIRL

The words to this song have gently plucked the heart strings (does the heart have strings? That's another book entirely) of many millions of music lovers since its release in 1994, so we do feel a little churlish questioning Tracey Thorn's claim that **I miss you like the deserts miss the rain**. But we simply have to ask one simple, penetrating question:

Do the deserts miss the rain?

It's a tough one. After all, deserts experience so little rain that you could leave Richard Harris's cake out in most of them for weeks or months on end without any soggy metaphors turning up to spoil it.

And yet we all want the one we can't have, so maybe the deserts are harbouring desperate desires for the rain based on the brief, tantalising encounters they have with it.

But surely, if you're a desert, you would grow up from an early age knowing that your life was pretty much mapped out for you in terms of rain, or lack of it, and if you spent your life pining for the few spots that occasionally fell on you, you'd be one terminally miserable desert. After all, the most you'd ever get would be an occasional one-night stand or the equivalent of a quick knee trembler behind the youth club disco.

Even if a desert who was missing the rain went to the most sympathetic therapist they could find – say, Dr Miriam Stoppard – she'd still feel duty bound to say, 'Listen Sandy, you've got to move on. The rain has, believe me.'

THE YEAR 3000
BUSTED

In this once-ubiquitous 2003 hit, the boy band trio, who specialised in what you might call 'trainer punk' (energetic guitar pop serving the same purpose as a trainer bra, and aimed at roughly the same demographic), claimed to have **been to the year 3000**, courtesy of a 'flux capacitor' as featured in the time-travel movie *Back To The Future*, and reported that **not much has changed but they live underwater**. Unlikely, you might think, but who are we to argue, without access to their boy band

Tardis? More alarmingly, especially for any parents who happened to bend an ear to what little Holly was listening to so obsessively, they also made approving reference to three-breasted women swimming around naked. Could they be entertaining dark groupie fantasies indulging all three band members indulging in some depraved soggy suckle-fest? Or is that just my own sick imagination? Then equally unlikely news comes in their boast that someone's **great-great-great-granddaughter is pretty fine**.

Clearly, female life expectancy and the average age of motherhood is going to shoot up in the next 991 years, if Busted are to be believed. If a teenage girl's future great-great-great-granddaughter was of a similar age in 3000, then she and her next four female antecedents would be giving birth to daughters at an average age of somewhere around the age of 197. Still, who knows what the future holds? Not Busted, who claimed elsewhere in this song they would be releasing their seventh album by this point, clearly anticipating Blue Nile-like gaps of around 140 years between releases.

They were either confident of eluding the ageing process or were dabbling in some of the Gallaghers' time-bending sub-stances. Either way, within two years they'd split up, and their Hitler-esque dreams of a 1000-year reign lay in tatters.

OH MY GOD
KAISER CHIEFS

Rock stars may be wealthy, worshipped and sexually irresistible, but that doesn't mean they don't feel the pain of you, the little people whose honest travails help pay for their quad bikes, designer sunglasses and divorce settlements. They understand only too well how **you work in a shirt with your name tag on it, drifting apart like a plate tectonic**. Or rather, they would, if they knew what a 'plate tectonic' was. Because even if we disregard the ear-chafing way they have made a Yoda-like word reversal of the more familiar geographical term, we have to ask: Does a tectonic plate drift apart, or do tectonic plates drift apart from each other? And when tectonic plates are most often in the news, during an earthquake, don't they push together?

They go on to empathise further with the bovine proles whose disposable income has made them millionaires. They depict the subject of the song **settling down in your early twenties, sucked more blood than a back street dentist**.

'Back street dentist'. The phrase rings a bell. Oh yes, that must be the equivalent of a 'back street abortionist', the oft-used term for an illegal, unqualified and quite possibly dangerous practitioner of pregnancy terminations, the kind which are common in countries where legal abortions are either difficult or impossible to come by.

Dentistry, at the time of going to press, isn't illegal anywhere in the world, and therefore you would have thought the 'back street' variety wouldn't be quite as in demand as their abortionist counterparts. Or even exist, in fact. Mind you, with our name-tag bound McJobs, I suppose we would be looking for an NHS dentist, and given their much publicised scarcity in recent years, perhaps a lucrative trade in unlicensed molar manglers really has sprung up.

But as for blood sucking – are vampire tendencies really that widespread in their industry? Injections, reclining chairs and Heart FM perhaps, but blood sucking?

Oh well, let's give them a break. Coming up with a rhyme for 'twenties' must have been very difficult. Like pulling teeth, in fact.

SWEAT
INNER CIRCLE

Many proud boasts have been made by musicians in the pursuit of provoking musical or sexual abandon (or preferably both) in the listener. So at first glance, this Jamaican reggae band's promise that **girl, I'm gonna make you sweat, sweat 'til you can't sweat no more** is a fairly orthodox statement of intent.

But on further consideration, this actually sounds faintly sinister. I mean, if she actually did sweat until she could sweat no more, wouldn't she be in a very alarming, life-threatening state of dehydration which would require hospitalisation? And you're saying you can 'make' her this way? Well, maybe you could offer your music to an establishment where such effects might be more welcome. It's called Guantanamo Bay.

JAILBREAK
THIN LIZZY

Tonight, announced Phil Lynott in this song's opening salvo, **there's going to be a jailbreak, somewhere in this town**.

I'm not the first person to point out that there's a prime candidate for the likely location of this jailbreak – the jail.

But that's assuming it's not a very large town. After all, if he was talking about London, the mass escape could take place at Wandsworth, Holloway, Wormwood Scrubs, Pentonville, Belmarsh or Brixton. Still, a few extra guards on duty on the night in question should nip the uprising in the bud, surely? Especially now you've blown the gaff and told everyone about it, Lynott, you slag!

AFRICA
TOTO

This unforgettable early-80s gem is invariably included on softrock compilations, but it also has won a place on many a list of lyrical misadventures, chiefly due to the bit where they observe that **as sure as Kilimanjaro rises like Olympus above the Serengeti, I need to cure what's deep inside.**

Many of you will have learned about similes and metaphors during secondary school English lessons. To recap for those whose attention may have wandered, a metaphor is when you compare two things by replacing one with something else (e.g.

Toto were giant bepermed love panthers bestriding the world of FM rock), a simile is when you say one thing is *like* something else (e.g. Toto looked like the queue for post-op counselling at a gender realignment clinic).

This line almost falls into the latter category, were it not for one important error. Even if you didn't listen, and think Simile is Chelsea's latest Italian transfer target, you will know that to say, as Toto have done, that Kilimanjaro rises like Olympus, is to say that a mountain rises like . . . a mountain. It defeats the object somewhat.

We can only shudder at the thought of how different some great works of literature would have turned out if previous writers had taken this resolutely unimaginative approach to comparisons.

'Shall I compare thee to a summer's day? No, thou art more like a dead-fit lass who I'd really like to get into the pants of.'

It's just lacking something, isn't it?

WALKING ON THE MOON
THE POLICE

When Sting, The Police's chief lyricist, imagined walking on the moon, and opined that **I hope my legs don't break, walking on the moon**, we had to wonder why such a self-styled intellectual would be worried. Of all the ailments that might possibly befall an astronaut, you'd have thought that broken limbs would be pretty far down the list. After all, with only a fraction of the gravity to deal with and pretty advanced footwear, padding and a spacesuit to protect you, there should be few such problems. Even an impromptu game of space football with a very unruly team of Clangers would be unlikely to pose any dangers in that department, since sudden movements would be so difficult to execute in that atmosphere.

So all things considered, don't worry about your legs, Sting – maybe just brush up on your knowledge of rudimentary astrophysics.

WHENEVER, WHEREVER
SHAKIRA

This fragrant Colombian introduced herself to the world with a feisty statement of intent, in which she noted that it is **lucky that my breasts are small and humble so you don't confuse them with mountains**.

Is that really likely? Mountains, breasts . . . breasts, mountains. Apart from sharing a vague resemblance in shape, they really don't have a massive amount in common, do they?

Or could this be a Colombian thing? Have there been well-publicised incidents in her home country where hikers have set out to conquer one of the Andes, and accidentally climbed up a woman's outsized breasts? Could she be making a wry reference to that incident? Or is she just making a really, really rubbish joke?

IRONIC
ALANIS MORISSETTE

Sooner or later, most successful performers end up having mixed feelings about their best-loved songs. They may have paid for three houses and a decade's supply of chang, but having to play them at every single show you ever do for the rest of your career, and have people singing them across the road at you while you're trying to buy tampons, can grate a little. Alanis Morrissette must be the ultimate example of that syndrome – she writes a bunch of songs as a teenager about having one hand in her pocket and the other one going down on someone in a theatre – or something along those lines – and 30 million records and 15 years later, people are still taking the piss.

Top of the ridicule charts from that album is this 1994 hit. It hardly feels necessary for me to point out its main fault, since I'm sure there are Japanese soldiers hiding out in foxholes, unsure if World War Two is over, who nevertheless know that 'Ironic' by Alanis Morissette is not very ironic. As many before me have noted, most of its observations are merely annoying, or frustrating, in a wait-half-an-hour-for-a-bus-and-three-come-at-once kind of way. But let's consider how we could potentially remix this lyric, to 'ironicise' it, if you will. So how about . . .

1) **It's like rain on your wedding day** *when you're the Managing Director of 'Weddings In The Sun – making dream days the weather can't spoil!'*

2) It's like ten thousand spoons when all you need is a knife *and you are the inventor of the 'spife', a special multi-purpose eating utensil that doubles up as both spoon and knife?*

3) A traffic jam when you're already late *for a meeting about the importance of timekeeping in the town planning industry?*

4) It's a no-smoking sign on your cigarette break *at a laboratory which tests out cigarettes' harmful effects on poor defenceless bunny rabbits?*

I could go on. But the quality control might dip a little, and we wouldn't want poor-quality spoof lyrics in a book about crap lyrics, now would we? That really would be . . . annoying.

KING LEER
MORRISSEY

Anyone reasonably well acquainted with his output to date will know that, contrary to his reputation as the messiah of miserablism, Morrissey does possess a healthy sense of humour. But everyone tells a duff gag now and again, and on this 1991 song, he left everyone smiling politely, repressing a groan and shuffling slowly away when he sang, **Your boyfriend he went down on one knee. Well could it be, he's only got one knee?**

No, it couldn't, Moz. If he only had one knee, he would have quite a bit of trouble going down on it, and even if he could that would make him an amputee and disabled jokes are kind of ... actually, on second thoughts, I suspect the ever mischievous Morrissey may well have been attempting not just a joke, but a double entendre, in the style of his beloved *Carry On* films, albeit one that is so creaky it has surely already snapped in two. Was he, perchance, hoping listeners would get the cheeky, 'oo er missus' double meaning of 'went down'? How queer!

Anyway, I say, I say, I say! My wife went to the West Indies!

SHOULD I STAY OR SHOULD I GO?
THE CLASH

As we saw in Thin Lizzy's talk of jailbreaks, some problems posed in song are more easily solved than others. Let us conclude this chapter with the conundrum offered by Mick Jones of The Clash, when he sang about a problematic relationship. **Should I stay or should I go now?** he asks. **If I go there will be trouble,** he confesses, but **if I stay it will be double**.

OK, let's weigh up the options ...

Go = trouble.

Stay = double the trouble.

So go then. Doh!

FIVE INCREASINGLY REDUNDANT SUBJECTS FOR SONGS

1) WAR

What is it good for? Well, historically it's been quite effective for imposing your country's will on another, but as a topic for a song, it's increasingly hopeless. Maybe in the 60s it seemed like quite a radical statement to highlight the futility of war, but in this day and age it sounds more akin to advising people that it's best to look both ways before crossing the road. If you can avoid sounding either over-earnest, patronising, morbid (yes, death metallers who write songs about people getting their limbs blown off, that means you), or hopelessly naive, then you're probably writing about something entirely different.

See: The Cranberries – 'Bosnia', Black Eyed Peas – 'Where Is The Love?'

CHAPTER 3

DOES YOUR MOTHER KNOW?

Inappropriate sentiments and woefully outdated attitudes

All of us from time to time entertain thoughts that would not meet with the universal approval of our peers. I, for instance, fantasise about aiming a fierce slap round the tanned, hairless chops of the delightful 14-year-old Olympic diver Tom Daley. But I never tell anyone, because I know I will never do it, and people may well think worse of me.

But hey, Rock'n'roll is outlaw country, so maybe I should write a song about my Junior-Olympian-slapping fantasies. After all, if there's anywhere that you can say the unsayable it is through the medium of popular song, right? Well, that's the theory anyway.

In reality, of course, some listeners might find the simmering subtext (or just simmering text, come to that) of violence against children to be offensive, and I would find myself forced to resign from songwriting and give my royalties to children's charities as journalists from the *Daily Express* grilled my parents on how they could ever have given birth to such a monster.

But who knows – maybe the tune would be so sublime that no one would notice the words. After all, some of the following songs are still regularly heard despite relaying the kind of messages that might, in different circumstances, have resulted in pressure groups picketing the BBC and demanding that they pay for everyone who heard the songs to have them surgically cleansed from their memory.

YOUNG GIRL
GARY PUCKETT & THE UNION GAP

It might be very difficult for someone to release a record now which addressed a young lady with words such as **Beneath your perfume and make-up, you're just a baby in disguise, and though you know that it's wrong to be alone with me that come-on look is in your eyes**.

Still, at least he acknowledges he's in the wrong with that memorable chorus of **Young girl, get out of my life, my love for you is way out of line. Better run, girl, you're much too young, girl**.

However, in the 21st-century moral climate, I suspect that within days of its first radio aring, Mr Gary Puckett's home address would be published on the internet, and a torch-carrying mob would descend on his house in Basingstoke, threatening to string him up from the nearest lamppost for even daring to express such taboo sentiments. His property would be daubed with misspelled insults and his car windscreen smashed, which would be all the more unfortunate since the Gary Puckett who wrote the song now lives in Florida.

DOES YOUR MOTHER KNOW
ABBA

I bet you were just waiting for these notorious Scandinavian filth-mongers to be featured in this chapter, weren't you? They present a similarly awkward scenario, with Bjorn singing,

You're so hot, teasing me, so you're blue but I can't take a chance on a chick like you.

Quite right, sir. But he can at least wax lyrical about her undeniable youthful charms, when he sings, **there's that look in your eyes, I can read in your face that your feelings are driving you wild, but girl you're only a child**.

Once again there's the suggestion here that these young girls are lust-filled temptresses, who are desperate (as any woman of any age naturally would be) to sleep with the fella with the pea-green dungarees and bowl cut out of ABBA. Or even the chubby one with the beard. Then again, this was the 1970s, when pea-green dungarees, bowl cuts and beards added up to a planet made of sex. Still, unlike other ABBA hits, at least this song isn't still being played today to millions of people in a Broadway musical and a Hollywood film. Oh, hang on . . .

AQUALUNG
JETHRO TULL

A multitude of lyrical sins can be accounted for by the old stand-by, 'They're not my words, I was describing a character'. Jethro Tull lyricist Ian Anderson would probably also argue that he had his tongue firmly in his cheek, and even now, these gnarled prog-rockers would probably avoid a visit from Her Majesty's constabulary, despite lines like **Sitting on a park bench, Eyeing little girls with bad intent**. But they might find airplay a little hard to come by with passages such as **Snot running down his**

nose, greasy fingers smearing shabby clothes. Drying in the cold sun, watching as the frilly panties run.

In hindsight, you probably didn't need to provide all that detail, Ian. And perhaps next time you perform it you could do an updated version, which describes how the character described is '*watching as the frilly panties run and a baying mob approach after reading about his recent move to the area in the pages of the* News Of The World'.

It's A Man's Man's Man's World
JAMES BROWN

The authors of other verses in this chapter would doubtless point out, with some justification, that at the time they were written, social attitudes towards such trifling matters as sexism, racism and intercourse with children were considerably different. For instance, James Brown was probably regarded as displaying quite a progressive, chivalrous view of the fairer sex when he made the observations that **Man made the cars to take us over the road, Man made the trains to carry heavy loads . . . This is a man's, a man's, a man's world**. You might think that an unenlightened viewpoint even by 1960s standards, but wait! He then makes the qualifying point that while men were responsible for producing pretty much every last molecule of the modern world, **it wouldn't be nothing,**

nothing without a woman or a girl.

Thanks for that, James, but doesn't half the world's population still get a slightly raw deal from that appraisal? Are you familiar with the term 'damning with faint praise'? I mean, what exactly were these women, or girls, doing to make themselves so indispensable? Just standing around looking pretty, waiting for their men to come home from building skyscrapers and inventing the internet? Even the most obvious natural talent of women – to reproduce the men who make the cars, trains and electric lights – is not deemed worthy of a mention. Still, that lyric is practically a groundbreaking treatise of feminist philosophy compared to these next examples.

STRAY CAT BLUES
THE ROLLING STONES

Don't let the title alarm you too much – the Stones may have been pretty wild in their late 60s pomp, but as far as I'm aware, they didn't include any animals in their sexual experimentation. They're not out of the woods yet though – the 'strange stray cat' they speak of would appear to be a young girl, who Jagger greets with the words **I can see that you're fifteen years old. No, I don't want your I.D.**

Why, that's very open-minded of you, Mick, thanks. He shows further hospitality later when he invites her friend to 'join in too', adding that it's not a 'hanging matter' or a 'capital crime'. Weren't the 60s wonderful? Such a gloriously innocent time.

Folklore has it that on their subsequent US tour, Jagger changed the lyric to 'thirteen years old' – just his cheeky little joke, you understand. And of course, all this is fiction – surely the Rolling Stones didn't really indulge in sex with under-age girls? Bill Wyman was unavailable for comment at the time of going to press.

HE HIT ME, AND IT FELT LIKE A KISS
THE CRYSTALS

Hmmm. Where do we start with this one? The title pretty much spells out the problem. And singer Barbara Alston justifies the actions mentioned therein by pointing out that **if he didn't care for me, I could have never made him mad, but he hit me and I was glad**.

Maybe the song's real-life origins might lend some mitigation. Or not, as the case may be. Husband & wife songwriting team Carole King and Gerry Goffin got the idea for this song after their babysitter, 'Little Eva' Boyd, told them about her relationship with an abusive boyfriend. She insisted he only hit her because he loved her. The resulting song, however, sung in the first person, features singer Barbara Alston admitting she had 'been untrue', thereby suggesting that she somehow deserved to be hit.

Phil Spector, the group's producer, svengali and noted

champion of women's rights (this was a man who used to insist his wife Ronnie Spector drove around with a blow-up doll version of himself to fend off potential suitors) insisted on its release, against the group's wishes, but even back in the more innocent age of 1962, listeners were outraged, and the single was soon denied airplay. Still, every black eye has a silver lining, and it did at least inspire an infinitely superior song title in the shape of Spiritualized's 2003 track 'She Kissed Me (It Felt Like A Hit)'.

HONG KONG GARDEN
SIOUXSIE & THE BANSHEES

Punk rock never had any truck with petty social rules or niceties. Yet when Siouxsie sang, **Slanted eyes meet a new sunrise, a race of bodies small in size**, she seemed to be expressing a knowledge and empathy with immigrant peoples that had more in common with pre-punk figures such as, say, Bernard Manning. **Chicken chow mein and chop suey**, they rhymed questionably with **Hong Kong Garden takeaway**, displaying all the searing wit of the bloke who goes into a Chinese restaurant and asks for 'flied lice'. But let's not be too hasty in our condemnation. After all, Miss Sioux has since claimed that the song was 'kind of a tribute' to immigrant communities who were harassed by skinheads in the late 80's.

It's certainly an interesting way of showing respect for other cultures, especially coming from a band who once wore swastikas on stage. I'm sure they meant well, though. Anyway, I'm off down the Notting Hill Carnival dressed in an afro wig and boot polish – it's my tribute to the afro-caribbean commmunity. I'm hoping for a warm reception.

Every Picture Tells A Story
ROD STEWART

Once The Beatles had taken the world by storm, the globe became a playground for tight-trousered troubadours eager to export some culture (usually a culture of sexually transmitted bacteria) to their foreign cousins. But like latter-day Marco Polos, they did at least report back on their experiences, to educate us in the customs and peoples they met there. As Rod Stewart put it in this postcard from the edge:

On the Peking ferry I was feeling merry, Sailing on my way back here.

I fell in love with a slit -eyed lady, By the light of an eastern moon,

Shanghai Lil never used the pill, she claimed it just ain't natural

. . . and so I did the decent thing, and put a condom on my Deng Xiao Ping.

OK, so I kind of made up that last line. But don't dismiss old Rod for any lack of chivalry, or indeed romance. He goes on to inform us how she won his heart, then refers to her once more as the 'slit-eyed lady'. How she must have loved that pet name.

Sadly, history does not record whether she affectionately dubbed him 'parrot face' in return.

GIRLS
THE BEASTIE BOYS

You know The Beastie Boys now as enlightened Renaissance men with a passing interest in eastern philosophies, but back in the mid 80s they thought it would be a hilarious jape to act as if they were semi-retarded frat boys with all the intelligence and sensitivity of adolescent bonobo monkeys [1]. They summed up their attitude with the charming lines **Girls! To do the dishes! Girls! To clean up my room! Girls! To do the laundry!**

They were, of course, being 'ironic'. Except they later admitted that they soon found themselves becoming exactly the kind of meatheads they had once intended to mock. Lead MC Adam Horowitz is now married to former Riot Grrrl pioneer and hardcore feminist Kathleen Hanna. Something tells me that this one doesn't get many airings when they're flicking through the family albums.

---

[1] Notoriously highly sexed members of the primate family. The Russell Brands of the jungle.

Play That Funky Music
VANILLA ICE

He was a lyrical poet, in case you didn't know it, but I don't think we could really include fascist sympathies among Vanilla Ice's many crimes. Yet he was surely asking for trouble when he wrote, **Now you're amazed by the VIP posse, steppin' so hard like a German Nazi**. Given his impeccably chiselled, blond, Aryan looks, we are forced to confront the nightmare of an army of Vanilla Ices annexing the Rhineland, not to mention rocking the mike like a vandal and cookin' MCs like a pound of bacon. Thankfully it didn't happen on this occasion, thanks to him being dropped by his record company for being an international laughing stock. But people, we must be forever vigilant that we never again give a platform to such evil madness.

FANTASY SONG TITLES TOP TEN: FASCISM

1. Seven Neo-Nazis Of Rhye
2. She Comes In The Falange
3. Needles And Pinochets
4. This Ole House Arrest
5. Know what Amin?
6. Papa's Got A Brand New Gulag
7. She's The One Party State
8. Oh What A Night Of The Long Knives
9. Jumping Someone Else's Trains That Run On Time
10. I'd Like To Teach The World Ethnic Cleansing

In The Summertime
MUNGO JERRY

Life was more carefree back in 1970. Video nasties hadn't yet been fully invented, only rock stars took drugs, and you could leave your front door open. You might get robbed and your house wrecked by rampant teenage delinquents, but you could if you really wanted to.

Mungo Jerry's perma-grinning, sideburned singer Ray Dorset was briefly the poster boy for this joyous universe when he wrote, **In the summertime when the weather is fine, you can stretch right up and touch the sky ... have a drink and a drive, go out and see what you can find**.

Can you spot the deliberate mistake in this lyric, readers? That's right, there's no way a human being would be able to literally stretch right up and touch the sky. And anyway, is the sky something tangible, which one can touch in any meaningful sense?

OK, maybe it was that second line that caught your attention, about having a drink and a drive.

This was, of course, 1970, when people could drive under the influence of drink without any ill effects (people could hold their ale in those days), so you can't really blame Dorset for including that carefree couplet.

However, he then continues on his theme, and openly advocates other serious acts of wanton law-breaking, suggesting that you **speed along the lane, do a ton or a ton and twenty-five** and later, **Make it good in a lay-by**.

Honestly, didn't he realise he was an important role model

to young people? It was bad enough sporting a pair of the most titanic sideburns in the history of facial hair, but to recommend travelling at 100 or 125 miles per hour along what is evidently barely even an A-road, let alone a dual carriageway, is surely incitement to the kind of speeding that would endanger both lives and driving licences. And as for his little roadside suggestion, indulging in sexual activity in such a public place is a sure-fire way of finding yourself up in front of the beak on a charge of outraging public decency. Worse still, other couples might approach them in the mistaken belief that the lay-by was a popular spot for 'dogging'[1]. So if you're listening to this record in the modern era, be sure not to take its suggestions literally. Have a drink (but not more than two pints or you're officially binge drinking), have a drive (but not at the same time, and remember to wear a seatbelt), go out and see what you can find — let's just hope it's not a drunk man with ludicrous facial hair being cut out of his overturned car at a notorious accident black spot.

[1] For those readers unacquainted with suburban sex practices, this reputedly involves voyeuristically inclined motorists driving to pre-arranged spots in order to observe other couples enjoying intercourse in their cars, and sometimes joining in. No one has ever actually witnessed this except Stan Collymore [2].

[2] Depressed former Premiership footballer who claimed that in the depths of his despair, he indulged in the activity described above, presumably attempting to alleviate his existential crisis by masturbating onto strangers' windscreens. Not to be confused with Stan Cullimore, former Housemartins guitarist, a perfectly happy man and, as far as we know, sexually as straight-laced as they come. No pun intended.

A Man Needs A Maid
NEIL YOUNG

Neil Young has a voice that naturally lends itself to yearning emotional resonance. When he sings, he emits a gentle, strangely soothing whine, which immediately invokes empathy, even on the occasions when he sounds alarmingly like Kermit The Frog singing 'Halfway Up The Stairs'. This song from his classic album *Harvest* starts off in a familiar melancholic vein, but then you realise he's singing about housework.

I was thinking lately I'd get a maid. Find a place nearby for her to stay,' he simpers. OK, that's fair enough. You're not short of a few bob, you're not in danger of transgressing any employment rules, and you're demonstrating an admirable concern for your employee's well-being. **Just someone to keep my house clean**, he continues, **fix my meals and go away**.

We can't really argue with that. But then we come to the chorus. **A maiiiiiiid . . . a man needs a maid,** he sings longingly, with more emotion than you might expect for someone who has come home to find stagnant washing up and pubes in the plughole. He later bleats, **When will I see you again?** so this must have been a maid with particularly formidable scouring skills. Yet I doubt his heart is aching for want of some light dusting and the loading of the washing machine. Either he has confused this maid with a romantic companion, or he has failed to make any distinction between a female partner and an unpaid domestic servant. Maid? Wife? They're evidently one and the same in Neil's world.

But Neil, what will you do if she actually wants to talk to you, maybe enjoy some quality time together as a couple, or possibly cuddle up in front of the telly watching *New Tricks* when you've got more important things to do, like sing about your bandmate's heroin overdose? Send her back to her place nearby? Shut her in the coal cellar?

And ultimately, what exactly was your message for womankind here, Neil? I'd guess at something along the lines of 'Keep on rocking in the free world . . . and by the way, love, my socks need darning.'

CHAPTER 4

LOOK FOR THE PURPLE BANANA

Utter nonsense

It is customary for songwriters to excuse their more impenetrable lyrics by explaining, 'It means whatever you want it to mean'. And there's me, naively thinking art was a form of communication. Let's just be thankful songwriters were never in charge of inventing our language, or you'd be saying, 'Good morning and how do you do?' and someone could legitimately interpret it as 'Will you please throw me off a viaduct?'

But while some of the songwriters mentioned in this chapter will doggedly insist that there is a method in their madness, in most cases I suspect they're way past caring if their emissions make sense to man or beast. In summary then:

This chapter is mostly just nonsense.

Let's hope it puts some paint on your conscience.

AROUND THE WORLD
RED HOT CHILI PEPPERS

If a picture paints a thousand words, then the challenge for a song is surely to write a picture in just a few short, singable lines. So it was a case of 'close, but no cigar', when Anthony Kiedis wrote the words to this 1999 album track.

Fox hole love, pie in your face, he quacked, sounding like Falco[1] having an asthma attack while trying to remember the words to 'Rock Me Amadeus', **living in and out of a big fat suitcase**. Wow, we've already flitted from some kind of porno war zone to the *Tiswas* studio, to a hotel room. But surely, this being the Red Hot Chili Peppers, an allusion to sex must be on the horizon.

Bonafide ride, he obligingly offers, **Step aside my johnson. Yes I could in the woods of Wisconsin**. Honestly, Anthony – you and your johnson.

Wake up the cake, it's a lake she's kissin' me. As they do when, When they do in Sicily.

Yes, they do do that when they do in Sicily, don't they? Those crazy, cake-waking, lake-kissing Sicilians. And like the rest of the world, they inexplicably buy Red Hot Chili Peppers records in their millions. I despair.

---

[1] Deceased Austrian 'rapper' who sounded like Anthony Kiedis coughing up a wishbone.

FEEL IT
THE TAMPERER (FT. MAYA)

It's the question that many a man has asked himself when in the first flush of romance with a new female partner. She may be beautiful, great company and you both enjoy philately and constant weight-free diving, but . . . **What's she gonna look like with a chimney on her?**

Indeed. Imagine the shame if you go to that all-important fancy dress party, and she goes as a three bedroomed Victorian house – only she looks an absolute dog's breakfast because of that chimney on her.

Your friends will surely shun you, you will never be able to look her in the eye again, and you will regret the day you ever met her. And yet, if she'd gone in that fantastic outfit dressed as a combine harvester, like you suggested, none of this would have happened. Women, eh?

BIKE
PINK FLOYD

Far be it from this book to preach to you about the evils of hallucinogenic drugs. After all, we are regularly told by those who have experimented that they have gained priceless insights into the secrets of the universe and all who inhabit it. What kind of insights? Well how about these, from noted gourmand of mind-altering chemicals, Mr Syd Barrett?

I've got a bike, he says, **You can ride it if you like**. He then tells us that it has a bell and a basket. He goes on to boast that he also has a cloak 'it's a bit of a joke', and a clan of gingerbread men. But best of all . . . **I know a mouse and he hasn't got a house. I don't know why, I call him Gerald**.

Tremendous! Mister drug dealer, sir, I'll have what he's having!

Cutt Off
KASABIAN

There's nothing more frustrating than someone telling you a story and then not getting to the end of it. This surreal tale from the Leicester rabble rousers starts promisingly, with the information that **John was a scientist, he was hooked on LSD, interested in mind control, and how the monkey held the key.**

Brilliant! You've got a high-concept pitch for a prime-time TV thriller series right there.

I can see John the acid-addict scientist now, using mind-altering chemicals to help solve all manner of grisly crimes with the help of his monkey sidekick, like a psychedelic Quincy. Not entirely sure how his drug use would affect the credibility of later testimony in court, but who cares, it's fiction, right?

But then, rather confusingly, he **said that all life is experiments someone's planning for the heir, it's for the unsuspecting citizens who hallucinate in fear.**

No, we're losing the plot here. Surely 'John' must be

getting heat from the DA, who doesn't like his maverick methods, and doesn't want him dabbling in police business?

Apparently not, because the next thing we're told is **aaaah, aaa-aaah aaaaah aaa-aaaaah chew the backbone, a solar system, these clever convicts.**

No, we're all at sea now. This is primetime drama, not bloody Dennis Potter! Run that past us again?

aaaah, aaa-aaah aaaaah aaa-aaaaah chew the backbone, a solar system, these clever convicts.

Oh God. People on drugs are never half as interesting as you expect them to be, are they? Just kind of boring and irritating. At least if they'd sung, 'Look at the orange pips – HA HAAA! they're climbing the clouds to heaven! EURGH! DON'T TOUCH ME! I'm unclean!' we'd know 'John' was tripping and would have left him alone.

Bicycle Race
QUEEN

If Queen had limited this song to concern only the irrepressible desire of wanting to 'bicycle', we wouldn't have had a problem, even if the image of Freddie Mercury dressed in full leotard bombing down a hill on his five-speed racer is an unlikely one.

But what was that random stuff he was barking on about in the verse?

You say 'black' I say 'white', You say 'bark' I say 'bite',
You say 'shark' I say 'hey man! *Jaws* **was never my scene**

And I don't like *Star Wars*.

What is this, some sort of bad-tempered word association game?

Well, I say tomato, and doubtless you say tom-ay-to – in which case, let's take it outside, tough guy.

He's not listening.

You say 'Rolls' I say 'Royce', You say 'God, give me a choice!'

You say 'Lord' I say 'Christ', I don't believe in Peter Pan, Frankenstein or Superman, all I wanna do is bicycle.

OK, well be my guest. There's this friend of mine called Syd, and he's looking for some company. Don't let him give you any sweeties, though.

BOHEMIAN RHAPSODY
QUEEN

Songwriters! Is writer's block squashing your imagination like a hedgehog on a motorway? Feel like writing a load of freeform gubbins, but fear the scorn of your peers? Well why not explain it away as 'operatic parody'? Freddie Mercury did, and the resulting song is often voted the greatest of all time.

How we failed to laugh knowingly at the complete absence of references to *Aida*, *Swan Lake*, *La Traviata* and *The Magic Flute* as Mercury sang **I see a little silhouetto of a man, Scaramouche! Scaramouche! Will you do the fandango?**

How we didn't chuckle as he declined to pastiche *Madame*

Butterfly, *Carmen* et al by singing **Thunderbolt and lightning – very very frightening me!**

And how we laughed out quiet when he stingingly mocked none of Mozart, Bizet or Verdi with the words **Galileo! Galileo! Galileo! Galileo! Galileo! Figaro magnifico!**

Oddly, the nano-genre of opera parody has pretty much lain dormant since this record was made. Who'd have thought it?

You Are The Everything
REM

Has Michael Stipe just been teasing us all these years? He spent a good decade of his career writing impenetrable oddness about fables of the reconstruction and sleeping sidewinders, or just-short-of-meaningful statements like 'Oh, life is bigger, bigger than me, and you are not me'. And then he suddenly comes out with a simple, transparent, heart-breaking lyric like 'Everybody Hurts', as if he was perfectly capable of conventional human communication all along.

This song from the album *Green* is classic Stipe, as he observes it is **Late spring and you're drifting off to sleep, with your teeth in your mouth**.

You don't say? Next you'll be telling us you're 'Sitting in a chair, with my hands on the end of my arms' . Or 'I'm hearing sounds with my ears'. Or 'I've got my spine, I've got my orange crush'. Actually, that last one rings a bell . . .

LET'S GO CRAZY
PRINCE

When people talking about 'going crazy', they usually mean it metaphorically. They don't mean 'Let's develop dangerous paranoid delusions in which our close relatives are trying to poison our food because they object to our imminent marriage to the Olympic rower and television personality James Cracknell'.

However, a committed eccentric like Prince perhaps knows more about madness than you or I, so when he sang, **Let's go crazy, let's go nuts. Let's look for the purple banana, until they put it in the truck**, perhaps he was referring to a specific bout of schizophrenia he himself had suffered, in which he actually felt driven to look for this elusive purple banana, and find it before it was removed in a truck by the government.

Or perhaps, as often turns out to be the case when obscure language is used, he's referring to his penis. Although if it's gone purple, then it's not just his mind that needs urgent medical attention.

SUPERFUNKYCALIFRAGISEXY
PRINCE

Further worrying evidence that the purple one was a Boutros short of the full Ghali back in his mid-80s prime comes in this writhing funk blow-out from *The Black Album*. He instructs his dance partner as follows: **Keep the blood flowin' down to your**

feet, Brother Lois will be around in a minute, with a bucket filled with squirreled meat.

I've been witness to a lot of strange sights on dance floors across the globe, from live sex shows to Harold from *Neighbours* attempting to 'jack his body'. But I must confess that buckets of meat are a new one on me. I suppose if it was kebab meat or chicken wings we might just about put it down to a quirky local custom. But 'squirreled meat'? Is that non-specific meat that's been 'squirreled' into the establishment? Or the flesh of an actual squirrel? If it's the latter, why squirrel? Does it have secret stimulant qualities? Is this some ancient tribal ritual? Either way, what are the chances of getting on the guest list for the next squirreled meat night?

Thorn Of Crowns
ECHO & THE BUNNYMEN

Just as New Order managed to carve out a highly respected career despite their lyrical crimes, Echo & The Bunnymen got away with some utterly bewildering old knackers while remaining in situ at the very peak of Mount Cool. Consider, if you will, **You set my teeth on edge. You think you're a vegetable, never come out of the fridge. C-c-c-cucumber! C-c-c-cabbage! C-c-c-cauliflower!**

Either he's reporting on a garden fete for the Stutterers Association of Great Britain, or he's making it up as he goes along. Mind you, Bunnymen singer and lyricist Ian 'Mac'

McCulloch rarely makes sense at the best of times. You'll surely recall the poignant tale of 'the cutting cutter' (see 'The Cutter'), and the touching talk of 'kissing the tortoise shell' ('Seven Seas'). And who would dare to answer the question 'I've got a barrel of shit, what do I do with it?' ('Do It Clean').

Well, if in doubt, Mac, write a song about it.

LOVE PLUS ONE
HAIRCUT ONE HUNDRED

Nick Heyward's clean-cut gang of popstrels were jovially cutting a swathe through the charts back in 1981 when this record stopped a generation of pop pickers dead in their tracks, as he sang, **I went off to the right, without saying goodbye. Where does it go from here? Is it down to the lake, I fear? Ay ay ay ay ay ah, ay ay ay ay ay ay ay ah.**

We were left to ponder eternally – just what was so fearsome about that lake?

If only they had explained the serious subtext of this song, and that this lake he was referring to was in fact Lake Nyos, a volcanic stretch of water in Cameroon, which has regularly pumped out deadly toxic gas killing thousands of people over the years. But no, they kept their counsel, and history laughs at them still, cruelly forgetting their neat pop songs and snazzy jumpers.

CHEEKY SONG
THE CHEEKY GIRLS

Criticising this song feels a little bit like slapping a deaf child for not listening properly. After all, I doubt this duo ever harboured ambitions to be the first twin female poet laureates. Still, even the words of Black Lace records seem to resemble vaguely common human sentiments, albeit those of a 48-year-old divorcee from Barnsley. The Cheeky Girls, on the other hand, simply have this to say:

Come and smile, don't be shy. Touch my bum, this is life.

This is life? Just that? My God, what a prospect. You're born, you touch people's bums, and then you die.

And thus we imagine a day in the life of a Cheeky Girl:

7am   wake up, touch bums.

7.15am   drink blood of virgins, touch bums.

7.25am   greet bizarre mother by touching her bum.

7.30am   truck arrives with daily consignment of 1986 vintage make-up and fake tan. Exchange bum-touches with bewildered driver.

7.45am   put on make-up, touch bums.

8am   breakfast – one apple pip (steamed).

8.30am   exercise, concentrating on gluteal (bum) muscles.

9am   English lessons (including bum touching).

12pm   lunch – one grain rice (steamed).

1pm   singing lessons (bum touching included).

3–7pm   do nothing except stare into space while touching each other's bums.

7pm   go out for bizarre dinner (one teaspoon cabbage soup, steamed) with bizarre cartoon-chinned Liberal Democrat MP. Touch his bizarre bum.

9pm   bum-touch mum goodnight. Climb into coffins.

FANTASY SONG TITLES TOP TEN:

LAKES

1. WE BUILT THIS TITICACA (ON ROCK'N'ROLL)
2. THE WINDERMERE BENEATH MY WINGS
3. GIRLFRIEND IN LAKE COMO
4. GENEVA IN A BOTTLE
5. NOW MY HEART IS ULLSWATER
6. HOW CAN I LIVE WITHOUT CHEW VALLEY LAKE?
7. ANOTHER BRICK IN THE WOLLASTON
8. BASSENTHWAITE — HOW LOMOND CAN YOU GO?
9. WHAT A WASTWATER
10. RESERVOIR FRIENDS ELECTRIC?

SHE WILL BE LOVED
MAROON 5

As a songwriter, you've got a fair bit of poetic licence. You can say someone has got golden hair, or eyes like diamonds, or ears like flattened baby mice, and no one will nit-pick too much at your description. Except me – I'm the nit-picker general, and I am here to ask these Californian pop-rockers just what they meant when they told me to **Look for the girl with the broken smile**, they crooned, **ask her if she wants to stay awhile**.

Broken smile? Has she got a hairlip or something? Plastic surgery gone horribly wrong? Leslie Ash's evil twin? I'm picturing some kind of walking Picasso painting, all crooked teeth and misshapen mouth.

I'm happy to look for her, if you insist, but once I've introduced myself with the words 'Ah, you must be the girl with the broken smile', I would imagine the question 'Would you like to stay awhile?' might get a fairly frosty response. You might as well say, 'I'd know those boss-eyes and Jimmy Hill chin anywhere. Fancy a bunk-up, love?'

And besides, it's not all that useful as a description for anyone 'looking' for her. 'Yes, officer, she's about small-to-average-to-tall height, with a broken smile. You can't miss her.'

Dktr Faustus
THE FALL

No book about questionable lyrics could be complete without the inclusion of Mark E Smith, a man who pretty much invented his own language in which to launch scattershot rants about whatever itches needed scratching in his ever-irritable psyche. He also regularly displays a tendency to arrange words as if they were bingo balls being spat randomly out of a machine. So we give you **Doctor Faustus: Horseshoes splacking swallows hay-cart, cart-horse of the peasant blocking his path.**

He starts off recognisably enough – *Doctor Faustus* is of course a Christopher Marlowe play based on the folk tale of Faust, who sells his soul to the devil for power and knowledge.

But . . . 'splacking'? Is that a word in the English language? Well, preliminary research reveals that, according to the urban dictionary, it means 'to get some (sex)'. Have his dabblings with the devil led him to attempt sex with swallows? Or a haycart? Or some swallows on a haycart? And where does the peasant come into the equation?

At least the fog begins to clear on the later passage, where he observes, **Must leave his student friends. FAUSTUS! Come get yer chips! Pull me blood silhouette, through the ceiling sky.**

Actually, on second thoughts, don't worry about decipher-ing that. Just give him 50p to buy some more Tennents Super and he'll probably go away.

Human
THE KILLERS

Some lyrics are born daft. Some achieve daftness (see the out-dated attitudes on show in Chapter 3), and some have daftness thrust upon them (by pedantic gits like me picking holes in them to highlight logical flaws). With this line, it was definitely the first one. An instant classic of the absurdist genre was born when Brandon Flowers sang **I'm down on my knees, searching for the**

answer . . . Are we human or are we dancer?

Well, whatever the answer is, I doubt you'll find it on the floor, as if it was a lost contact lens. But then, what exactly is the question? It would surely have meant no less to man or beast if he'd asked, 'Are we human or are we next Friday lunchtime?' or 'Are we human or are we Modern Pentathlon?'

But then Flowers publicly explained the line by claiming it was a reference to a Hunter S Thompson quote about 'a generation of dancers'. Right. Well, I have on occasion felt quite inspired by Mark E Smith, but if I walked around barking 'Come get yer chips!' apropos of nothing, I might struggle to get my point across. Unless of course I had fallen on hard times and had taken a job as a streetcorner chip-seller.

Anyway, I'll have to stop there. I'm feeling a bit donkey[1].

---

[1] In case you're too stupid to get this reference, it's from a passage in the Dead Sea Scrolls where one of the disciples says, 'I feel as sick as a donkey who has just carried the fattest man in Judaea across the desert'.

FIVE INCREASINGLY REDUNDANT SUBJECTS FOR SONGS

2) REAL BEAUTY IS ON THE INSIDE

Narrowly edging out 'It's not the winning, it's the taking part' for the title of most patronising saying in the English language, this is an increasingly common theme in modern-day songwriting, and like most other condescending tripe, it's always a) bloody easy for them to say, and b) sounds as sincere as bailed out CEOs saying they always believed there was a place for government intervention in the banking industry.

The songs which feature this theme will invariably be performed by artists airbrushed to the point where they'll soon need an emergency tracheotomy to avoid suffocation, and girl bands who you know for certain would once have chewed their bandmates' noses off just to get a walk-on part in *Byker Grove*, and would gladly undergo enough plastic surgery to turn a giraffe into a dachshund in order to meet whatever puddle-shallow criteria of physical perfection currently holds sway.

So there is surely a gap in the market for someone to say something along the lines of:

'Beautiful on the inside? Have you seen my insides? They look like Freddie Krueger after falling into a mincing machine. They're foul. Not a lot of beauty in there, either, I'm afraid . . .'

See: Christina Aguilera – 'Beautiful', TLC – 'Unpretty'

CHAPTER 5

SQUEEZE MY LEMON

*Outrageous sexual innuendo and
bad euphemisms*

Considering the very phrase 'Rock'n'roll' is said to have once been slang for making the beast with two backs, it's hardly surprising that sex has been a popular lyrical topic in popular music since back in the days of the blues. However, in the interests of good taste, lyricists have often sought to couch the subject in euphemistic terms. The trouble is, sometimes they lack the poetic sensibilities to, erm, pull it off . . .

The Lemon Song
LED ZEPPELIN

Robert Plant, Jimmy Page and co were never backward in coming forwards when it came to matters of courtship. In fact rock folklore has it that they showed all the sensitivity in matters of romance of Cro-Magnon men at the end of a particularly epic night on the peyote. But when they copied the line from Howlin' Wolf's 'Killing Floor' and instructed an unnamed partner to **Squeeze my lemon 'til the juice runs down my leg**, many a sensitive gentleman winced at the very notion.

After all, it's surely a pretty dangerous instruction for a man to give to his sexual partner. Any man who has had the pleasure of their other half treating their pride and joy with all the tender loving care of a mediaeval municipal water pump will shudder at the prospect of someone squeezing their 'lemon'. In fact, the most likely 'juice' to be forthcoming from such a technique would be from the poor fella's watering eyes.

Let Me Put My Love Into You
AC/DC

When metal's most supreme riff merchants sing **Let me put my love into you babe, let me cut your cake with my knife**, there's an undeniable fingernails-down-a-blackboard effect. Yet it does allow us to make a fairly all-encompassing rule that all future songwriters should observe: Under no circumstances should you use the word 'knife' in a seductive context. No matter how kinky your sex life might be, and regardless of how imaginative your fantasies may be, if you've reached the point of opening up the cutlery drawer, it's time to call Relate.

Other pointy objects may be permissible for metaphorical use, however. For instance, you might wish to reassure a nervous partner by saying, 'Nothing to worry about, although you may feel a bit of a prick'.

NAKED
EXTREME

Musicians have never been strangers to boasting about their sexual prowess, but relatively few operating outside the braggadocio tradition of hip-hop have actually felt the need to spell out the, erm, full extent of their charms. So consider, if you will, these Boston rockers' words **You want me to take it off, just to see what's underneath my cloth. I'll show you I'm every inch a man – measure all that you think you can**.

If you'll allow me to offer my own admittedly radical interpretation of these lyrics, I'd suggest that he's talking about someone measuring his penis. The fact that he's suggesting that task is beyond us can only mean that the appendage is of a size beyond all human understanding. Some kind of four-dimensional space penis perhaps? An ever-mutating, shape-shifting super-knob that defies all classification? All the more reason to keep it under wraps in that case . . .

Pour Some Sugar On Me
DEF LEPPARD

As the legendary *Viz* cartoon character Finbarr Saunders (he of the double entendres) demonstrated, it is possible to read euphemistic intentions into the most innocuous of phrases, if you so desire. But some such linguistic devices found in popular song seem to completely miss the point of the exercise, and leave even the most perceptive and worldly connoisseur of slang searching in vain for any relation to any recognised human sexual activity.

This invitation from Sheffield's finest to **Pour some sugar on me, in the name of love**, is surely a case in point. What could they possibly be referring to by 'sugar'? Some bizarre form of water sports? Food sex? Role play as mating cornflakes?

Or perhaps we're reading too much into this. Maybe they do want a woman to quite literally pour some sugar on them, in the name of love. As opposed to, say, 'pour some sugar on my cornflakes, in the name of a tasty and nutritious breakfast'. But it wouldn't half make a mess on the sheets.

And he's not finished yet, as he growls, **You got the peaches, I got the cream.**

No, mate, that's for pudding – one meal at a time, you weirdo!

KINKY REGGAE
BOB MARLEY AND THE WAILERS

My giddy aunt, this lot are at it too. **I went downtown**, says Bob, **I saw Miss Brown.**

She had brown sugar all over her booga-wooga. Are we missing something with this sugar business? Are there people all over the world having hours of private fun with the same stuff we God-fearing folk are putting in our tea? And another thing: maybe some readers of Caribbean origin can confirm otherwise, but I suspect that the word 'Booga-wooga' doesn't have any official meaning either in English slang or Jamaican patois. But, unlike some other nominees in this chapter, at least they're not asking anyone to measure it.

THE JOKER
STEVE MILLER BAND

It can't have been easy chatting up a potential mate back in the 1970s. This was, after all, the era of *Carry On* films, when it seems that everything had to be wrapped in painfully laboured euphemisms. If you wanted to instigate foreplay on your wedding night, you couldn't come out and say it, you had to try something like, 'Can I, erm, have a twiddle at your dials, darling, and see if I can find Radio Luxembourg?' Or so my dad tells me at any rate.

So perhaps we should take our hat off to Steve Miller, who was fairly forward on this 1972 hit. **You're the sweetest thing that I ever did see**, he cooed. OK, not particularly original, but it might have an initial effect on the easily impressed. He continues, **Really love your peaches wanna shake your tree. Lovey dovey lovey dovey lovey dovey all the time. Ooh yeah baby I'll sure show you a good time**.

Right. And peaches would be . . . a reference to the young lady's buttocks perhaps? Or bosoms? Well, surely that's a little previous at this stage. And 'lovey dovey lovey dovey'? *Que*? Shouldn't the baby talk start a good few months into the relationship – rather than as part of a chat-up line? As for the 'good time' part of the equation, judging by the taste displayed in the previous two lines, I can't help but wonder if your idea of a good time would be a visit to Hooters followed by a request to dress up in a nappy.

SISTER
PRINCE

In this sensitive 1981 paean to the joys of sex with a sibling, Prince tells us **My sister was 32, lovely, and loose. She don't wear no underwear, she says it only gets in her hair. And it's got a funny way of stoppin' the juice**.

He later observes that 'Incest is everything it's said to be.' Having never tried it, and having no intention of ever doing so, I'll have to take his word for it. But one drawback is that sex with a sibling clearly has a devastating effect on your dress sense – why on earth would anyone want to put underwear on their head? Or does he mean . . . oh, I see. Hmmm . . .

LOVE RESURRECTION
ALISON MOYET

We'd be frankly disappointed if we bought an AC/DC record and it didn't contain at least a couple of blatant double entendres. But you don't always expect to find such thinly veiled filth in the work of MOR warblers like La Moyet. So we can only assume she's talking about gardening when she sings **What seed must I sow to replenish this barren land?**

Well, get your hands on whichever seed takes your fancy, but make sure the area where you're planting is nice and moist, which allows nice deep planting.

Teach me to harvest, I want you to grow in my hand. OK, well you've certainly stimulated my interest there. But keep at it. Don't stop now. Don't stop, or you could lose what growth you've achieved thus far.

For a warm injection is all I need to calm the pain. Well, I'd advise against the use of chemicals. As long as the bud looks nice and bulging when it pops up, you should be well on your way, and you'll have spectacular, satisfying results in no time.

YOU REMIND ME OF SOMETHING
R KELLY

It's generally considered acceptable in polite society to refer to one's car in the female third person, e.g. 'She's still a reliable little runabout, the old girl.' But it doesn't really work the other way round. Someone should have pointed that out to lascivious soul frotteur R Kelly before he wrote **You remind me of my jeep (I wanna ride it)**.

Really? What are you going to do? Try and have your wicked way with the exhaust pipe?

Somethin' like my sound (I wanna pump it). There's electrics involved, I'd leave well alone, especially if you're a bit sweaty.

He then takes objectification of the female form to absurd extremes when he coos, **Girl you look just like my car (I wanna wax it)**.

Does she really look like a car? Is she 12 feet long with alloy wheels?

Somethin' like my bank account (I wanna spend it baby).

Really? Does a message flash up when you're 'making a deposit', saying, 'Please take your penis and wait for your orgasm?' Is she open at weekends? And what are the charges like?

Burn Bitch Burn
KISS

Rock bands do come up with some unlikely topics for songs, such as Kiss's use of a real log fire in this romantically named love ballad. **Oh babe,** groans Gene Simmons, **I wanna put my log in your fireplace**.

That's fine, as long as you put it in gently – you don't want your 'log' spitting everywhere. And make sure the fireguard's up – children and household pets sometimes become inquisitive and stick their paws in.

Star Girl
MCFLY

I bet you were just waiting for these notorious sleazehounds to make an appearance in the filthiest depths of this tawdry tome, weren't you? And they haven't let us down. The pick of their many depraved hymns to deviancy is this tale of loving an unnamed mystery girl from another planet. **Hey girl**, they drool, **there's nothing on earth could save us, when I fell in love with Uranus.**

At least that double entendre is so subtle that it might just fly over the heads of some of their younger, more suggestible fans. If they happen to be particularly slow. And unable to read and write. Or hear.

My Humps
BLACK EYED PEAS

Regarded by many as the 'Bohemian Rhapsody' of euphemistic nonsense songs, this jaw-dropping paean to singer Stacey Ferguson's allegedly 'lovely lady lumps' takes objectification of the female form to sewer-like depths.

Whatcha gonna do with all that junk? asks rapper Will.I.Am, ever the silver-tongued poet of seduction, presumably intending it as some cack-handed compliment.

I'm gonna get, get, get you drunk, replies Fergie. **Get you love drunk off my humps**.

What are you, some sort of camel?

My hump my hump my humps, she continues. **My lovely lady lumps**.

If Will.I.Am was remotely sane, he would be feeling a little unsettled by this point, wondering if he'd picked the woman who lives in the bus shelter and eats bird droppings as a chat-up target. And then she really hits the self-destruct button. **I'm gonna make, make, make, make you scream, Make you scream, make you scream. Cos of my hump, my hump, my hump, my hump, My hump, my hump, my hump, my lovely lady lumps. Check it out!**

Call me over-cautious, but I think by this time I'd suddenly be remembering an urgent appointment overseas.

Yet she's met her match in Will.I.Am. He's lapping it up! And after already setting new standards for leery sleaze and gut-churning single entendres, he raises the bar higher still, with the following gibbering soliloquy:

I mix your milk wit my cocoa puff,
Milky, milky cocoa,
Mix your milk with my cocoa puff, milky, milky rlllllllght.

....

....I'm sorry, I had to pause there. Words failed me for a few stunned moments. In the absence of an expert in hip-hop slang here, I can only speculate that 'cocoa puff' and 'milk' are meant to somehow represent the sexual union of a black man with a white woman. Represented through the use of the kind of metaphors that most primary school children would consider lacking in sophistication, if not downright racist.

The song carries on in much the same vein. And you should hear the b-side to this one, a scorching hip-hop cover of 'I've Got A Lovely Bunch Of Coconuts'. Saucy!

CHAPTER 6

THAT BOOK
BY NABOKOV

*Intellectual pretensions, over-reaching ambition,
and impenetrable cryptic twaddle*

Rock'n'roll used to be an innocent place, where even London School Of Economics students like Mick Jagger would rather imitate the unlearned tongue of a Mississipi cotton-picker than show off the fact that they had a half-decent set of A-levels.

However, by the late 1960s, when even Mickey Dolenz was requesting an audience with the Maharishi, scores of musicians – even a few drummers – were keen to show off their interest in eastern philosophies and radical politics, and tackle weighty subject matter through the medium of song. All leave was cancelled for the poetry police from thereon in.

By the time 'progressive' rock had thrown a hefty jewelled cape over the musical landscape, and vaguely mystical science fiction such as Tolkien had become required reading, this pseudo-intellectual cancer had become a faux-profound plague. And Sting wasn't even famous yet.

All seemed very proud of their self-improvement. But pride comes before a fall, or at the very least, comes before song lyrics with all the grace and emotional resonance of a man slurping a Pot Noodle on a tube train.

Unless, of course, you the humble reader can succeed where millions have failed, and decipher some deep and lasting truths from the following passages. As James Joyce himself probably once said to someone about something at some point: 'Best of luck'.

BALLAD OF A THIN MAN
BOB DYLAN

Countless influences have been deemed partly responsible for 'dumbing down' our precious popular culture, but when it comes to who 'clevered it up' in the first place, we can slap a large dollop of the blame on the big-nosed bard from Hibbing, Minnesota.

His way with words has been compared to every great figure in the history of literature (with the possible exception of Pam Ayres) and there's no doubt he lent new poetic depth to folk and rock alike. But listening to a song like this, you wonder if his reputation was enhanced by the fact that everyone thought he was way too cool to ever be guilty of obscurantist gibberish, but was in fact imparting cryptic pearls of wisdom, and it was up to us to decipher their meaning.

This celebrated anthem for a generation is a case in point. Not content with accusing the 'Mr Jones' everyman character of having 'contacts among the lumberjacks' (Ouch! Go easy with your satirical scythe, Bob!), he then rhymes 'imagination' with 'tax deductible charity organisations', and tells of a sword swallower in high heels who has borrowed someone's throat. You can imagine presidents and prime ministers crumbling under the polemical weight of such metaphors, can't you? But the best is yet to come, as he spits:

Now you see this one-eyed midget Shouting the word now
And you say, for what reason? And he says, 'how?'
And you say, what does this mean? And he screams back,
'you're a cow'
Give me some milk or else go home.

Inspiring stuff, all allegedly ridiculing the confusion of the 'straight' world in the face of the brave new generation of whom he was a figurehead. And ridiculing the confusion of everyone else, in fact by, erm, confusing them with ridiculous words. In fact just writing it all down has inspired me to compose my own message for the disaffected youth of the 21st century:

> *The fair-headed chaffinch is shouting 'Mind the mines'*
> *and trying on a policeman's hat that chimes.*
> *You say 'Where's your chicken liver paté?'*
> *And he says 'in the Bay Of Biscay'*
> *before retiring to the internet café*

Stitch that, Gordon Brown!

RAMBLE ON
LED ZEPPELIN

After beginning their career singing almost exclusively about women who done them wrong and shamelessly rewriting old blues numbers, Led Zep clearly needed some fresh lyrical inspiration on their second album, the imaginatively titled *Led Zepelin II*. It came in the shape of JRR Tolkien's *Lord Of The Rings*, a post-war children's fantasy novel. **'Twas in the darkest depths of Mordor,** claims Plant, **I met a girl so fair. But Gollum and the evil one crept up and slipped away with her.**

Of course we can all relate to the idea of being stuck in a mythical land on an epic quest to find some sort of ring, when a satanic force (say, Darren Day?) runs off with your new girlfriend. And this was just the start of Plant's interest in fantasy. As yet, however, even the finest literary minds have struggled to pin down the passage in Tolkien which might have given him and his bandmates the idea for the infamous meeting between a female fan and a fish in a Seattle hotel room.

21ST CENTURY SCHIZOID MAN
KING CRIMSON

Now we are nicely settled into the 21st century, safe in the knowledge that the world didn't stop working due to a computer bug on Millennium Eve, it's easy to laugh when we look back at predictions of what this century might hold. But King Crimson lyricist Peter Sinfield should have known he was taking a risky punt back in 1969 when he wrote **Cat's foot, iron claw, Neurosurgeons scream for more at paranoia's poison door. 21st century Schizoid man!**

Although the noughties are yet young, I would sincerely hope medics won't reject modern technology and return to the use of cats' feet and iron claws in the pursuit of brain surgery, just as I wouldn't advocate the throwing of women in ponds to see if they were witches.

And while a 21st-century schizoid man might well find himself at paranoia's poison door, he'd surely have every reason to be worried if he was being given neurosurgery instead of psychiatric treatment, and the people operating on him were having screaming fits and suffering from bouts of mental illness themselves.

No such problems for Sinfield, evidently, as he went on to write 'The Land Of Make Believe' for Bucks Fizz. Couldn't he have persuaded someone to perform a bit of screaming neurosurgery on them too?

In The Year 2525
ZAGER AND EVANS

For all we know there could be plenty of 26th-century schizoid men walking around in half a millennium's time, but these 1969 futurists saw a rather simpler vision.

Ain't gonna need to tell the truth, tell no lie. Everything you think, do and say is in the pill you took today.

Really? And what about taking the pill itself? Did I do that of my own free will? Or did the pill I took yesterday make me wake up today thinking, 'I really need to take my pill today?' In which case, what made me start taking the pills in the first place? Another pill taker? And where are these pills coming from? Do they get delivered to my house by the government? And who is driving the delivery van? Is his pill telling him to make deliveries of pills to people? In which case, has he been given a different kind of pill? And by whom?

I could do with a few pills myself after such brain-aching considerations, but we must crack on. The song certainly does, at a rough rate of 1010 years per verse, and the future will develop further still, according to our soothsaying one-hit wonders.

In the year 4545, ain't gonna need your teeth, won't need your eyes. You won't find a thing to chew, nobody's going to look at you.

Well, no, because they presumably won't have any eyes either.

We are then promised that by 5555, we won't need arms or legs, because 'some machine' is fulfilling those functions. Crikey. So, without the power of sight, traditional foodstuffs or ability to eat, will humanity be evolving, or regressing into some sort of amoebic state?

At least things are looking up slightly by 6565, because by that time, we're told, we'll pick our sons and daughters from 'a long glass tube'. And yet, that's not really much use, is it? At this rate I'm going to be sat in 'some machine', a blind, unthinking lump of blubber, with the 'pill' having already decided I'm going to have a slightly rotund, unathletic son called Darryl and an anorexic jug-eared daughter called Esme. Great.

And so a simple futuristic scenario plunges us into a whole philosophical and logical can of worms. What's the chances of a pill which would return pop to the simple pleasures of 'I Wanna Hold Your Hand'?

A Passion Play
JETHRO TULL

Despite the aspirations of progressive rock songwriters towards high art, they were still sleazy, skirt-chasing reprobates at heart, and so often they just couldn't resist letting their base instincts get in the way. No doubt Jethro Tull's bulbous-eyed, storm-haired flautist and chief lyricist Ian Anderson was, once again, just joking when he sang **And your little sister's immaculate virginity wings away on the bony shoulder of a young horse named George who stole surreptitiously into her Geography revision**.

We are bound to ask, though: If this girl is 'your little sister', then just how old is she supposed to be? The fact that she is evidently of school age might not come as any great surprise to anyone reasonably well acquainted with the sexual politics of ill-shaven early-1970s rock stars, but if he is suggesting that her first sexual experience was with a beast of the field, then I find myself wondering if Mary Whitehouse ever had the pleasure of giving this magnum opus the once-over. Oh, and Ian Anderson now owns a successful trout farm in Scotland. Considering the bestial fantasies he has already outlined, do you think it's worth a call to the RSPCA? Or Led Zeppelin, for that matter?

THE REVEALING SCIENCE OF GOD
YES

Although few people could make any sense of the random pronouncements made by the prog-rock icons responsible for *Tales From Topographic Oceans* (literally meaning 'tales from the blue bits on a map'), singer and lyricist Jon Anderson clearly felt he had a hotline to the man upstairs.

The Lord works in mysterious ways, but he obviously chose Jon to reveal some of his less palatable thoughts about the world he created, and inspired Anderson to warble, **Craving penetrations offer links with self-instructor's sharp but tender love as we took to the air, a picture of distance**.

Aaaall together now! Crrrr-raving penetrations offer links with self-instructor's . . .

OK, maybe it's not ideal singalong material. So perhaps it's more suited to serious intellectual analysis. For me, the 'penetrations' he mentions can only be referring to some kind of construction work, and 'self-instructor's sharp but tender love' must surely be some kind of drill. He's saying God is desperate for some drilling by the lead singer of Yes. Well, aren't we all?

THE WIDTH OF A CIRCLE
DAVID BOWIE

The man known to his mother as David Jones has undoubtedly had a massive influence on several generations of musicians, and it's not hard to see why when he sings:

I ran across a monster who was sleeping by a tree, and I looked and frowned and the monster was me.

Well, I said hello and I said hello, And I asked 'Why not?' and I replied 'I don't know'.

So we asked a simple black bird, who was happy as can be. And he laughed insane and quipped 'KAHLIL GIBRAN!'

Oh, to have been a fly on the wall (or possibly a nearby park bench) when all that took place. A skinny bloke in a woman's dress (or I presume so from his appearance on the sleeve of *The Man Who Sold The World*, the album whence this song comes) conducts a conversation with himself, then attempts to include a blackbird in their discussion, only for it to make a philosophical in-joke and collapse in gales of mirth. Then later in the song, you'll be interested to learn, he has sex with the devil. Like you do.

Rock fans the world over can only breathe a sigh of relief that no psychiatric professionals were nearby during this encounter, or Bowie might have been carted off to the funny farm there and then, and the history of British pop music would have been much the poorer.

As it was, no doubt the nation's second-hand bookshops were later besieged by young pop pickers with feather cuts who had been inspired to buy Kahlil Gibran's *The Prophet*, only to find it didn't have half as many pictures as *Look-In*, and took a rather dim view of men dressing up as women and licking their guitarist's crotch on stage.

DON'T STAND SO CLOSE TO ME
THE POLICE

As a musician, one naturally wants to be taken seriously. But at the same time, when you are an intellectual and Renaissance man of Sting's stature, it would be vulgar to show off about it too much. So he probably thought he was being relatively modest when he wrote in his story of a pupil's crush on a teacher, **He starts to shake, he starts to cough, just like the old man in that book by Nabokov**.

He is careful not to patronise us, assuming that we know exactly what book he is talking about – *Lolita* by Vladimir Nabokov. And yet there's something about the slightly forced way that 'cough' and 'Nabokov' are rhymed that betrays his utter determination to tell the world that he has read some dead clever books.

He might have got away with it if he had tried to rhyme something with 'Lolita' – How about *'She wants to learn but he'd love to teach her'*? *'She's wearing quite a tight swee-ater'*? *'Is it hot in here or have my trousers been fitted with a nuclear-powered heater?'*

No, all things considered, it's best to just steer clear of this minefield of a subject – Oi! Sumner! Leave those kids alone!

BLIND YOUTH
THE HUMAN LEAGUE

Before they became slanty-haired pop icons in the early 1980s, The Human League were a rather dour electronic outfit for whom the celebration of emotional austerity and granite-faced, quasi-Soviet iconatry was paramount. Yet their Kraftwerk-style sheen of robotic efficiency sometimes smudged a little, due to statements such as **Dehumanisation is such a big word – it's been around since Richard The Third**.

Maybe educational standards in South Yorkshire were a little on the shabby side back in 1979 when this song was released. So who can blame Ian Craig Marsh and Phil Oakey for considering the 14-letter word 'dehumanisation' to be big, when as the bloke on the corner table at your local pub quiz can tell you, antidisestablishmentarianism puts it to shame, at 28 letters long. And you can tell they're winging it when they come to the line about Richard The Third. In those days when the information superhighway was not even a public footpath, they probably imagined they could get away with such wild statements. But we can confirm that the word dehumanisation has definitely been found in scripts from the early Plantagenet era, and different spellings have been recorded in texts dating back to the Domesday book.

OK, fair enough, we're winging it too.

DEEP DARK TRUTHFUL MIRROR
ELVIS COSTELLO

Pop has never been shy of asking searching questions of its listeners. Why does it always rain on me? Does your chewing gum lose its flavour on the bedpost overnight? Are we human or are we dancer?

However, the man who once called himself Napoleon Dynamite may have struggled to get a response when he mused **A stripping puppet on a liquid stick gets into it pretty thick. A butterfly drinks a turtle's tears, but how do you know he really needs it?**

And that's just your starter for ten, pop pickers! . . . **'Cos a butterfly feeds on a dead monkey's hands. Jesus wept, he felt abandoned**.

I have to confess, so do I. One of the post-punk era's finest songwriters has apparently taken leave of his duty as an entertainer to take a long and pointless trip up his own fundament.

But let's not bow to our Philistine tendencies and dismiss his words out of hand. There are important questions thrown up by these lines. Do turtles cry? Does Jesus, for that matter? Do butterflies eat dead primates? Is FR Leavis in the house?

The answer would appear to be a simple 'no' on all those counts. Which leads me to conclude that while there may be some important TS Eliot-style symbolism in all this, creatively speaking, Elvis is ultimately just fiddling with his liquid stick.

CHAPTER 7

HIP HOP, YOU DON'T STOP . . . BUT MAYBE YOU SHOULD

Rhymes against humanity – Part Two

Rhyme is to rap what hip is to hop. The two are inextricably linked, like the actress Sarah Miles with the practice of drinking your own wee.

A rapper without a rhyme is like a cyclist without a cycle, but while the latter needs only one of his/her chosen tools, rapping is a wordy business that demands enough couplets on a single album to keep Chris Martin in business until 2071.

The law of averages dictates that the odd creaky combination cannot fail to slip into the repertoire of even the most ruthless of microphone fiends – witness the occasional discarded fridge that blocked the river of Rakim's highly-acclaimed flow (see Chapter 12). Meanwhile, the need to impress your peers with ever more exaggerated claims about yourself, and outlandish accusations about your rivals, can lead you to conjure up lines which scan like a photocopier with a paper jam. Here are a few from the archives. Sucker MCs take cover . . .

Part Time Sucker
KRS ONE

The old saying has it that those who can, do, and those who can't, teach. For all his undoubted skills, KRS One did seem to back up that theory when he wrote this tune about teaching lesser rappers how to rhyme.

A tool for holding water is a cup or pail, he says. **The opposite for fresh is stale, the largest sea-mammal is a whale. Beer is called ale, or sometimes it is called brew, a group of human beings is a crew . . .**

Thanks, Kris, sorry to interrupt you in mid-lesson. As it happens, some Ofsted inspectors are visiting your school of rap today, looking into falling educational standards. They'd like a quick word, if that's OK.

Dancehall
SLY AND ROBBIE FT. KRS ONE

KRS was kind enough to not only give his own lessons but perform guest lectures on other people's records. So when this legendary reggae production duo wanted to make a commercial rap record, they turned to Boogie Down Productions' main man. And just how pleased they must have been with their investment when he exclaimed, **If you're not a square and you do have hair, and every day choose your underwear, let me hear you sing 'oh yeah!'**

Despite his self-proclaimed academic credentials, KRS clearly didn't think that one through, and nor did his employers. Did they want people to enjoy their music? Or just a select few? Well, ruling out the entire 'square' population of the planet is not a good start. What if eminent squares like Ann Widdecombe MP or Sir Trevor McDonald had been listening to the song? And did Sly and Robbie also realise they were excluding Duncan Goodhew, alopecia sufferers, and underwear-eschewing celebs like Paris Hilton in their rallying call?

BACK TO THE GRILL
MC SERCH FEATURING NAS

You've got to big yourself up to earn 'props' in the respect-obsessed world of hip-hop. But you might want to make sure your claims sound vaguely convincing. On MC Serch's 'Back To The Grill', the east coast rhyme king Nas fell short on that score with his boast **This is Nas, kid . . . you know how it runs, I'm waving automatic guns at nuns**.

It's possible that being in the UK, I missed the blanket US news coverage of this notorious nun massacre of 1992, but I don't think I'm risking litigation if I say I suspect he was speaking 'figuratively', or, as they say in UK 'hoods, 'talking out of his arse'.

FIVE INCREASINGLY REDUNDANT SUBJECTS FOR SONGS

3) IMAGINARY WOMEN

There she goes, she's like the wind, she's so high, she's so heavy, and Sheena is a punk rocker. She is also a figment of your imagination, I'll wager. Male artists have frequently used a woman as a 'muse' to spur them into frenzied creation. But sometimes the female subjects they immortalise in song just don't quite have the ring of authenticity. I mean, just how many women called Mary has Bruce Springsteen ever known? Either he grew up next door to the National Headquarters For The Advancement Of People Called Mary, or there's a middle-aged woman in New Jersey who has been stalked in song by the same man for the best part of four decades.

See: Primal Scream – 'Country Girl, Blur' – 'She's So High'

Dwyck
GANG STARR

We see here a classic case of a job half-finished. An artist comes up with a line he feels is suitably powerful, and can't think of anything to rhyme it with. So he says **Lemonade was a popular drink and it still is. I get more props and stunts than Bruce Willis**.

I think you'll join with me in giving your 'props' to Guru, who came up with this jaw-dropping statement for the east coast crew in 1994. Now, I'm merely speculating here, but I suspect he came up with the Bruce Willis punchline, and needed a first line to be a mere stooge to set it up. Maybe he should have just ditched the first part altogether, just as he wisely did with his own name. Because Guru was originally known as Keithy E The Guru. Would you buy a used philosophy from such a man?

Know How
YOUNG MC

There's nothing technically wrong with making random remarks as part of your 'flow', but when you're using them in the pursuit of self-promotion, there's always the danger that you'll sound as impressive as a middle-aged schoolteacher showing off his new leather trousers. So it proved when this Boston rapper barked, **Always chillin', never illin', in my mouth I got two fillings**.

Damn! What else ya got homie? Double-jointed fingers? All your own hair? Hands that do dishes?

Still, at least we'll be able to identify him from dental records if he should ever get in a 'beef' with anyone. Or indeed, if he should accidentally wander past Nas when he's on one of his nun-shooting rampages.

EXPRESS YOURSELF
NWA

Speaking of 'beefs', it is not only *de rigueur* in the rap world to big yourself up, you also have to beat a few suckers down with the mic to earn 'respect'.

Our dearly departed friend Eazy-E of NWA was no stranger to the 'diss', and produced a pearler on 'Express Yourself' when he spat, **You ain't efficient when you flow, Movin' like a tortoise, full of rigor mortis**.

Well, we've heard of rappers claiming to be unafraid of death, or even predicting an imminent visit from the grim reaper, but if he's claiming that this person is actually rapping after having been dead for several hours, that's got to be a first. If only Eazy had been able to record him, he could surely have stunned the world, and given the circumstances, we could surely have overlooked the deceased vocalist's inefficient flow.

SUPERTHUG
NOREAGA

Diss your inferiors until your heart's content, but as a rule, it's hard to insult people if they don't understand what you're on about. This low-rent gangsta rapper comes a cropper on that score when he rants, **Yo, Light a candle, run laps around the English Channel, Neptunes got a cocker spaniel**.

He later explained that this was in fact a dig at the highly respected Neptunes production team of Pharrell Williams and Chad Hugo, and it was intended to suggest they were homosexual, due to their choice of canine companion.

We've heard of liking Barbra Streisand or dressing like one of the Village People as common signifiers of homosexuality, but cocker spaniels? Surely, if there was an award at Crufts for 'most sexuality-neutral breed', they would be running second favourite to the golden labrador.

From such neanderthal views, you'd never guess Noreaga was a bit dim, but that conclusion is backed up further when we consider the line about the English Channel. Clearly one cannot run laps round a stretch of sea that is not enclosed by land, and thus he has committed the worst crime in modern hip-hop – he has failed to keep it real.

If he could have stuck to more orthodox, credible claims based around murdering members of religious orders, we might have taken him seriously.

FANTASY SONG TITLES TOP TEN:

DOGS

1. You Can Call Me Alsatian
2. Fade To Greyhound
3. Something In The Airedale
4. Get Out Of Your Lazy Bedlington Terrier
5. Fly Like A Beagle
6. Jack Russell Your Body
7. Living In A Foxhound
8. Wherever I Lay My Flat-coated Retriever
9. The Pugs Don't Work
10. Addicted To Basset Hounds

21 SECONDS
50 CENT

Even the meanest of gangstas do occasionally show their sensitive side, with the kind of love poetry that would surely make Keats shed a small tear. We're not quite sure what kind of tear, but they all count.

'Fiddy' may have been shot nine times (although all in the same incident – why do people always say it as if it was in nine separate incidents and he's invincible, like he's the Rasputin of rap or something?) but he still has big love for 'da honeyz'.

Always remember girl we make mistakes, he says to a girl who he affectionately calls 'shorty', then offers **to make it up I do whatever it take – I love you like a fat kid love cake.**

Aww, you sure know how to makes a girl feel special! Even if you can't punctuates to save your life!

Then again, maybe these kind of lines only work for millionaire rappers. You should have seen the look my girlfriend gave me when I told her 'I love you like a coprophiliac loves being defecated on during the act of sexual intercourse'.

CAN'T NOBODY HOLD ME DOWN
PUFF DADDY FT. MASE

After conquering the world with his Bad Boy record label and Sean John clothing empire, the artist soon to be known as 'Oh, God, not him again' clearly felt somewhat omnipotent as he actually stepped up to the mic himself for his debut solo single. Maybe that's why he let his protégé Mase make the startling boast that they were **Young, black and famous, With money hangin' out the anus.**

It had long been fashionable in hip-hop to wear your trousers low slung, to display your expensive designer underwear. Thankfully, this even more blatant method of displaying one's wealth never really caught on.

Let's Get Ready To Rhumble
PJ & DUNCAN

You know them today as the family-friendly duo who have bestridden the world of early-evening family entertainment like a short, twin-headed colossus in recent years. But behind Ant & Dec's cheeky grins and knockabout banter lies a dark secret – rhymes so foul they have caused hardened songwriters of 20 years' standing to break down and weep.

A duo, a twosome, so many lyrics, we're frightened to use 'em, they barked. But clearly, they weren't frightened enough. **So many lyrics, we keep them in stores. We've even got them comin' out of our pores**.

So bearing that sweat-related information in mind, we can officially confirm – these lyrics stink.

Chapter 8

War Is Stupid

Well-meaning words, rubbish lyrics

I once had a lecturer at college who was blind. He was, however, determined to live as normal a life as possible, and he invariably walked around the campus with neither white stick, nor guide dog or human assistance to guide him. Most of the time he coped admirably, but I cannot forget the one occasion when he came a cropper.

Venturing outside during a lunch break, he seemed to lose his usually reliable bearings, and walked straight into a bike rack. He sprawled headlong over some panniers as bystanders rushed to assist him. I was initially one of the rescue party, but after an instinctive move towards him, I turned away, because I couldn't stifle my giggles in the face of such priceless slapstick.

I still feel bad about that, but they do say comedy is tragedy plus time. About four seconds, in that particular case. Likewise, when musicians insist on using their chosen medium to impart a serious message, and then deliver it with all the skill and effectiveness of Cristiano Ronaldo taking an air swipe at the ball and falling on his perfectly formed behind, they can hardly blame us for enjoying the action replay. I think the technical term is 'bathos'.

Similarly, the following examples of well-meaning polemic fall somewhat short of their noble aims. I'm sure they'll forgive us if we enjoy those moments again in glorious slow motion. With extra analysis from the studio.

PIECES OF YOU
JEWEL

On the title track of her multimillion-selling debut album, this ultra-liberal American singer and poetess took bigotry of every variety to task, and asked searching questions such as **You say he's a Jew – does it mean that he's tight? You say he's a Jew – do you want to hurt his kids tonight?** She goes on to mention his 'funny hat' and then concludes with the words, **Oh Jew, oh Jew, do you hate him, 'cos he's pieces of you?**

We know what she's driving at, and we sympathise but . . . but . . . did you ever see Rick in *The Young Ones* dreaming about being The People's Poet? ('Oh cliff . . . sometimes it must feel like you really are a cliff, when fascists try to push you . . . over the edge'). This is a marginally higher standard of verse, but there's something about the banality of the poetry juxtaposed with the blunt violence of the language just tickles you, like a puppy being squashed by a piano.

Just kidding.

ZOMBIE
THE CRANBERRIES

Around the same mid-90s era, Ireland's own answer to Jewel was The Cranberries' Dolores O'Riordan. It was the wrong answer, delivered with an insufferable yodelling voice reminiscent of Dana choking to death on a boiled sweet, but that didn't stop her alerting us to the ills of her homeland, as if two decades of news headlines wasn't enough. However, the impact of her response to 'the troubles' was slightly dampened by lyrics like **with their tanks and their bombs, and their bombs and their guns, in your head, in your head!**

You can imagine Martin McGuinness himself taking a moment to reflect, can't you? He probably thought, 'Why does she repeat the line about bombs? Are we using twice as many bombs as guns and tanks? Surely that's a serious strategic issue we need to be addressing.'

And she's not finished yet.

They are dying, she pleads, **in your head, in your head, Zombie! Zombie! Zombie!**

Not quite Martin Luther King's 'I Have A Dream', but I guess we get the general thrust of the argument. Then again, why is this 'in your head'? Is she suggesting the entire history of the troubles of Northern Ireland are the product of someone's fevered imagination? And where do zombies come into it? Are they a previously little-known splinter group of paramilitaries drawn from the living dead? Do they have a political wing?

It's very confusing.

I Just Shot John Lennon
THE CRANBERRIES

By the time of The Cranberries 1996 album *To The Faithful Departed*, Ms O'Riordan was feeling sufficiently fired up to address numerous global issues, from Bosnia ('Bosnia was so unkind') to war ('We should mind the war child'), to drugs ('To all those kids with heroin eyes, don't do it' – looks like they already have, Dol). But she excelled herself on this account of John Lennon's assassination. **It was the fearful night of December eighth, he was returning home from the studio late.** Fearful? I remember it being quite a balmy evening, actually, but on you go . . . **He had perceptively known that it wouldn't be nice**, she observes, **and in 1980 he paid the price**. The price for what, exactly? The price for knowing 'it' wouldn't be nice? That seems expensive to me. Anyway . . . **With a Smith & Wesson 38, John Lennon's life was no longer a debate**.

Debate? What debate? Oh, of course, only weeks beforehand, the Oxford Union was discussing the proposition: 'This house holds that John Lennon is not really alive, he's just a hologram, and while we're about it, isn't it possible that we are all actually just avatars in a giant computer program, have no free-will, and don't ultimately exist in any physical sense?'

EBONY AND IVORY
PAUL MCCARTNEY & STEVIE WONDER

On this famous plea to end world racism, the former Beatle and his illustrious collaborator made a touching comparison between black and white people, and black and white keys on a piano. The key message was, of course, **Ebony and ivory live together in perfect harmony. Side by side on my piano keyboard, oh Lord, why don't we?**

It's one to ponder, isn't it? In fact, where do we start? I suppose we could begin by pointing out that piano keys generally have no problem 'living' next door to each other because they are, by their very nature, pieces of ebony and ivory, and are therefore not sentient beings with brains, emotions, or free will. Therefore they don't feel racial prejudice towards other materials, or anything else for that matter. Once we've established that fact, we realise that in fact there's not a great deal of valid comparison to be made between piano keys and human beings.

But if Macca really is asking why we, black and white people, don't live together in harmony, you have to delve deeper. You could look back to the natural tendency mammals have for forming tribal groups, and their self-preservatory fear of anyone or anything they consider to be 'different' from them, then you could perhaps touch on the socio-economic divisions first established between races through the slave trade, and then you could look at the history of economic migration and consider how politicians have used notions of racial and national identity as a means to divide and rule, and then . . .

D'you know what? I'm thinking this might be too big a subject to tackle even in a weighty intellectual tome like this, let alone a few lines of a pop song. Best leave it well alone. Mr McCartney, sir, can I direct you to a chorus of frogs currently gathered by the garden pond?

If Everyone Cared
NICKELBACK

This heartfelt and thought-provoking plea for universal love and understanding presents the myriad of possibilities for the human race 'if everyone cared'.

If everyone cared, and nobody cried, he argues, and **if everyone loved and nobody lied, then,** it logically follows, according to lyricist Chad Kroeger, **we'd see the day when nobody died**.

Let's take that statement one sentence at a time.

Granted, it would be nice if everyone cared – the kind of bold, cut-the-crap statement that Jewel and Dolores would surely endorse. But no one crying? Isn't it universally accepted by doctors and psychologists as an important stress reliever and coping mechanism, without which our mental health could potentially suffer? And surely the world's greengrocers would be up in arms after the eradication of the onion from this brave new weep-free world?

Quite apart from that, does he have any scientific research to show how love, caring and the eradication of lachrymosity will eradicate death? Is he saying it will extend human longevity indefinitely, succeeding where many thousands of mad scientists, vampires and Michael Jackson have failed?

More importantly, would that be a remotely agreeable state of affairs? I feel confident in saying that if nobody died, within a fairly short space of time the world's over-population problems would reach such a crisis point that governments would have to implement radical, *Logan's Run*-style measures to keep the numbers down. If nobody died, they'd have to be killed. Unless, of course, Chad has further plans to give the human race a bit more 'Lebensraum'[1] and has another song up his sleeve called 'If We Could Then Go On To Colonise Mars'.

---

[1] Lebensraum, literally meaning 'living room', was Adolf Hitler's plan to invade foreign territories in order to make room for the expanding Master Race. Any relation between him and the singer from Nickelback is purely coincidental. Although they did both have highly identifiable facial hair.

IF THAT WERE ME
MEL C

The Spice Girls were never widely noted for their social conscience, and perhaps it's for the best that they preferred taboo-shattering statements such as 'Friendship never ends' and 'Mama, I love you' to broaching thorny subjects such as homelessness. However, as a solo artist Mel C evidently felt she was old and wise enough to put herself in the place of a destitute rough sleeper, and attempt to empathise with their plight. She felt moved to ask the question, **is it lonely where you are, sleeping in between parked cars?**

If Mel's vision is to be taken at face value, then homeless people's nocturnal habits have more in common with cats than human beings. It's a miracle that none of them have been run over by cars reversing out of parking spots oblivious of the homeless person sleeping inches away from them.

What's more, the neighbourhood of which you speak must be an area with a pretty anarchic approach to parking restrictions. I feel pretty confident that if I even so much as knelt down for 20 seconds in between cars to look for a lost contact lens, I'd be clamped by a ruthless team of tool-wielding council sub-contractors and my next of kin would be sent a demand to pay £50 to have me released on pain of a custodial sentence.

And would you do so much as a benefit gig to publicise my plight, Mel? Would you heck as like.

MELTING POT
BLUE MINK

For most of the 20th century, the debate about the ethics of genetic engineering has been raging. There has always been the fear that if the technology to alter the racial make-up of the globe became widely available, it could be used for practices such as eugenics, which the Nazis were once fond of in Germany.

These distinctly hippyish Californians clearly planned to use it to more benevolent ends, however. They suggested we **take a pinch of white man, wrap it up in black skin**.

They went on to coo over the prospect of **curly Latin kinkies, mixed with yellow chinkies**. A brave plan, but you have to wonder how everyone of East Asian origin would feel about being lumped together among the label of 'yellow chinkies'? And just what are 'curly Latin kinkies' when they're at home? Are all Latins curly? Or kinky, come to that, given the popularity of Roman Catholicism in such countries?

But hey, maybe we should just chill out. They later assure us that their racial mix (also including 'Red Indian boy' and 'blue blood' apparently) would mean **you've got a recipe for a get-along scene**. *Au contraire*, my friends, I think your programme of enforced inter-breeding would be a recipe for a series of nationalist uprisings, possibly culminating in a Third World War.

Stick that in your pot and stir it, you flower-haired fools!

THE WAR SONG
CULTURE CLUB

This is surely political pop boiled down to its supremely banal bones. As if we could ever forget the thunderous message of this 1982 anthem, it told us **War, war is stupid, and people are stupid, and love means nothing in some strange quarters**. That's right. All the thousands of years that people have fought over territory, religion, or to defend their land from invaders, they were just being 'stupid'. He may have a point in some cases but might I suggest he's being a touch simplistic in his appraisal? And as for the 'people' part of the equation, isn't that another slightly sweeping statement? Can he expand on it? Well, he does talk about people who 'fill the world with narrow confidence', whatever that is, and then mentions how we're 'fighting in the street, won't somebody help me?'

Well, probably not, possibly because they don't want to fight, because war is stupid. Twat.

TIME FOR TRUTH
THE JAM

In stark contrast to his modern-day image as a happy-go-lucky, twinkle-toed family entertainer and chat-show raconteur, the teenage Paul Weller was a pretty po-faced fella. The trouble was, sometimes he couldn't quite articulate his rage as eloquently as he might have liked.

For instance, on this tune from The Jam's debut album *In The City*, he sneers, **Whatcha trying to say that haven't tried to say before? You're just another red balloon with a lot of hot gas. Why don't you fuck off?**

No point beating around the bush, I guess. Later he takes another pot shot at this unspecified enemy. **What happened to the great empire? You bastards have turned it into manure**.

Well, I know parts of India are very smelly, but it's also very beautiful . . .

FIVE RIDICULOUSLY OVER-USED RHYMES

1) NIGHT / ALRIGHT

If we built this city on rock'n'roll, then several hundred bricks must have been consistuted from positive emotions associated with weekend leisure activities. Friday and Saturday nights, or indeed, 'tonight' in general, are almost invariably going to involve feeling 'alright'. But rarely any better than that.

'Alright' is such a resolutely underwhelming word. It's a real pity that we can't popularise an alternative couplet to express the fantastic feeling of a highly enjoyable experience during the hours of darkness. Personally, I'd like to see someone predict that 'on Friday evening we'll feel so good we'll be disbelieving' or 'By Midnight Friday we'll be getting slippy and slidey'. Any takers?

See also: Tight, bright, out of sight

2) FLY / SKY

You'd think that when songwriters imagine flying, a whole universe of opportunities would present themselves. So why is by far the most popular imaginary destination for songwriters, simply 'in the sky'?

I mean, it's nice and quiet and all, but there's not a great deal there. A few birds, some clouds, maybe an electrical storm if you're really lucky.

Wouldn't it be more fun to, say, fly down the stairs so the cat thinks you're a giant pterodactyl? Or up to the 21st floor of your old office to appear at the window of your old office like Banquo's ghost, and then rub your nose on the window to leave a mark, just in case they thought you were merely an celestial body or a terrifying hallucination.

At least Lenny Kravitz wished that he could fly 'High up in the sky just like a dragonfly', so presumably he could at least catch a few lesser insects to eat. As if there weren't enough in his hair already.

See also: High, why, my

3) AIR / CARE / YEAH

We know that it is impossible to wave your hands in the air, while also appearing to care. No, you must wave them like you just don't care. The song you're listening to is so powerful that you could throw yourself gleefully into some helicopter blades any moment, or try to eat your own knees. While saying 'oh yeah'.

It really is a wonder that there aren't more horrific accidents due to the care-free atmosphere at pop concerts.

See also: There, dare, hair

4) PHONE / HOME / ALONE

People in songs always 'call you on the phone'. As opposed to calling you via a skype video conferencing facility or by use of a series of whistled morse code signals.

Once they've done that, they're bound to find that you either aren't home, are 'alone' or, indeed, are 'not alone'. Couldn't they give us some more illuminating detail, and get offended at the fact you were eating a SCONE while talking to them? Or perhaps drama could ensue when they misinterpret your strident TONE, because they've been sitting around getting STONED all evening.

There, you can have those ideas ON LOAN.

See also: on your own, ignite your bones

5) DANCE / TAKE A CHANCE / ROMANCE

'She said "come on let's dance",' wrote Hard-fi in 'Hard To Beat', "we've got to take our chance"

Take our chance? Why, was she about to turn into a pumpkin? Or were they at some strange church dance where you were restricted to a five minute period of dancing per evening, outside which you were not allowed to interact with the opposite sex?

Singer Richard Archer later tells us 'That girl you saw round town, well now she's going down'. Honestly, Rich, what price a little 'Romaaance'? Chris De Burgh used it to woo his Lady In Red, and he's up to the back wheels in crimson-coloured action these days.

See also: Circumstance, hot pants

YES
MANIC STREET PREACHERS

These Welsh firebrands have often made Paul Weller look like Leo Sayer in the chirpy stakes, and their third album *The Holy Bible* may be the most mercilessly bleak record you will ever hear. And thrilling though it was at times to hear them, as one sample on this album put it, 'rub the human face in its own vomit and force it to look in the mirror', they didn't half spout some cobblers in the process.

They set their stall out on the opening track, in which they observe, **In these plagued streets of pity you can buy anything, for $200 anyone can conceive a God on video. He's a boy, you want a girl so cut off his cock. Tie his hair in bunches, fuck him, call him Rita if you want**.

Now, I know there were plenty of very bad things happening in the world in 1994, but I find it hard to believe that this was one of them. Maybe the Manics had been consuming news sources of a more unreliable variety to me, but even in Amnesty International's most harrowing reports, I have yet to hear of any countries where it has ever been common practice to perform DIY sex changes on your own children, even without combining it with rape and incest. Moreover, mutilating children would surely lead to major complications such as, well, death from blood loss or infection, which would surely defeat the object of the exercise, unless there are hundreds of surgeons prepared to attempt this exceptionally rare form of gender realignment surgery for the kind of bargain prices the song suggests.

SEXUALITY
BILLY BRAGG

Some people say you should keep pop and politics apart. I'd beg to differ. Popular music would surely be a poorer place without 'Free Nelson Mandela' if not The Family Cat's 1993 less successful polemic 'Bring Me The Head Of Michael Portillo'.

But mixing sex and politics? Well, you're on shaky ground. Billy Bragg almost would have got away with it on this cuddly 1990 hit if it hadn't been for an unfortunate juxtaposition. **Sexuality!** went the anthemic chorus, **Strong and warm and wild and free! Sexuality! Your laws do not apply to me! A nuclear submarine sinks off the coast of Sweden . . .**

Ouch. Just when we were getting our juices flowing with all that rugged talk of wildness, freedom and breaking the law, someone mentions nuclear submarines. What a passion killer. It's like you're just reaching second base with that special someone and they decide to switch off Barry White and turn on *Channel 4 News*.

As John Lennon so wisely put it, 'If you go carrying pictures of Chairman Mao, you ain't gonna make it with anyone anyhow'.

WE DIDN'T START THE FIRE
BILLY JOEL

It was always likely to be a thankless task attempting to shoe-horn half a century of world history into a four-and-a-half-minute pop song. And Billy Joel resolutely failed to do it on this bewildering list of post-war world events.

The song basically amounts to a rapid-fire list of buzz-words, as if he's grabbed a bag of those fridge magnets with world events on, stuck them on the door, and listed what came out. And when he makes bedfellows, of **Chubby Checker, Psycho, Belgians in the Congo**, or indeed **Lebanon, Charles de Gaulle, California Baseball**, you're left wondering if his list is any more profound than me listing things I did today.

How about *picked my nose, fed the cat, watched Cash In The Attic and had a difficult crap*?

Or *Bit my nails, bread's gone stale, Insulted a man in telesales*?

All of which are accurate glimpses into my daily existence, but perhaps don't offer much wider insight into the human condition.

The limits of this approach to history are summed up when he bellows **JFK! Blown away! What else do I have to say?!**

Well, a fair amount, Billy, since you ask. I mean, why no mention of the civil rights movement? The advent of the European Economic Community? Mark Spitz's unprecedented seven gold medals at the 1972 Olympics? Supersonic passenger flights? Matt Bianco getting called 'wankers' on *Saturday Superstore*?

Come to that, I know the 1970s are best forgotten but was it wise to cover the entire decade in the space of about eight words?

Apparently they sometimes play this record in secondary school history lessons. And they wonder why educational standards are going through the floor.

CHAPTER 9

BUT THEN AGAIN . . . NO

Chronic lack of inspiration

Even the most prolific of songwriters sometimes suffer from their muse pulling an extended sickie without a moment's notice. Nine times out of ten, they'll go away, have a ride on their private jet pack, take some liquid GHB, search their CD collections for an obscure melody to steal, and they get through it. Occasionally, however, it leads to a flagrant abdication of duty, either through utterly uninspired lines whose impact on the listener most closely resembles that of a soggy piece of toast falling to the floor (jam-side down, naturally), or transparent attempts to fill the gap with lines about . . . not being able to think of the next line (see p150 'Annoying things lyricists do').

YOUR SONG
ELTON JOHN

~~If that Elton John lyric was a bit~~ . . . no, let me rephrase that. ~~A more famous example of~~ . . . no, it's still not quite right. ~~Economy of language is all important in~~ . . . hang on, let me think about this.

It's infuriating, isn't it, to read something which is more like a rough draft than the finished article?

So how did Elton and Bernie think we'd feel about the line **If I was a painter . . . but then again, no . . .**?

What comes next? 'If I was a painter . . . what?' That's the question he leaves dancing on our lips. But judging by this example, it's a no-brainer. If he were a painter, he'd decorate half our front room, and then think 'nah . . .' and decide to take up carpentry instead.

DANIEL
ELTON JOHN

Bernie Taupin often did a grand job writing the words for Elton John to sing, but a less forgiving employer might have docked his wages on this occasion.

They say Spain is pretty though I've never been, offers Elton. **Well Daniel says it's the best place that he's ever seen. And he should know, he's been there enough**.

I've heard Croatia's nice. A friend went there recently and

they said it was lovely. A lot of people are buying houses out there at the moment, I've heard. Mind you, the language barrier's difficult, and they do like their wars round those parts, don't they. It's always a bit unstable. Got any plans for the weekend?

Do you see what I did there? That's right, instead of writing about this song, I substituted a random conversation I might have with my hairdresser. It doesn't really work, does it?

Bernie Taupin takes the same approach when writing these lyrics, with equally unedifying results.

I presume Elton must have quickly had a word, or his subsequent records would have included songs about how there's going to be a cold spell next week, do you know a reliable electrician, and did you see *Silent Witness* last night?

THE LEBANON
THE HUMAN LEAGUE

Sometimes you hear a lyric where you can't quite pin down the essence of its rubbishness . . . for some reason, it just reeks of 'wrong'. And that was the unmistakable scent that wafted our way when Phil Oakey sang **Before he leaves the camp he stops. He scans the world outside. And where there used to be some shops is where the snipers sometimes hide.**

I think the root of the problem is in the incomparable mundanity of the phrase 'some shops', in a song about a civil war in the Middle East. You can't help but picture a bullet-riddled branch of Spud-u-like, a rubble-strewn Dollond & Aitchison and

Pret A Manger advertising special sandwich-plus-drink deals for Druze & Christian Militia. Perfectly conceivable of course, but . . . then again, no.

FANTASY SONG TITLES TOP TEN:

SHOPS

1. DANCING WITH MY SELFRIDGES
2. JUST A LIDL LOVING
3. SPAR! (WHAT IS IT GOOD FOR?)
4. THE GREEN GREEN GRASS OF BRITISH HOME STORES
5. POUNDLAND OF MAKE BELIEVE
6. LAST NIGHT A DJ KWIK SAVED MY LIFE
7. LIVING DOLLOND AND AITCHISON
8. VISION EXPRESS OF LOVE
9. DOWN BY THE WATERSTONES
10. O SUPERDRUG

BEING AROUND
THE LEMONHEADS

In rock's great power vacuum of 1993, as grunge was grunting its last and Britpop was but a twinkle in Damon Albarn's pearly whites, The Lemonheads' Evan Dando was every girl's favourite indie pin-up. But he was displaying an increasing tendency to write ditties that sounded more suited to *Teletubbies* than *Top*

Of The Pops. And so it was that we were faced with the thorny question, **If I was a booger, would you blow your nose? . . . Would you keep it? Would you eat it? I'm just tryin' to give myself a reason, for being around.**

A generation thought about this little conundrum for a short while, then decided to wipe him on the underside of their desk and get on with their lives.

Highway Star
DEEP PURPLE

According to a deluded but powerful minority of recording artists, including such notables as R Kelly (Chapter 5), cars are a lot like women. Deep Purple seconded that motion with this 1972 song about a car that was a 'killing machine' which was going to 'break the speed of sound'. Although such a prospect was extremely unlikely considering the state of motoring technology in the early 1970s, they went on to boast of similar attributes enjoyed by their girlfriend.

Nobody gonna have my girl, brags singer Ian Gillan. **She stays close on every bend.** Is that strictly sensible if you're travelling at the speed of sound? Surely she'd want to stay at least two chevrons behind to avoid accidents.

Ooh, she's a killing machine, she's got everything. Like a moving mouth, body control and everything.

All those male readers whose girlfriends have bodies that just flap and flounder about uncontrollably, with mouths as inanimate as Barbie herself, will surely be green with envy. And most women couldn't murder a cup of tea, so the killing machine part is also a major bonus, in case you need any enemies taking out.

And what's that – ' . . . she's got everything'? And then everything AGAIN?!!

Actually, sorry mate, we were on your side for a while but now you're getting cocky.

S.Y.M.M.
MANIC STREET PREACHERS

That title stands for 'South Yorkshire Mass Murderer', since you ask. Not always a popular number at wedding discos and family gatherings, but it made it onto the Manics multi-platinum album This Is My Truth, Tell Me Yours in 1998. And considering it refers to the Hillsborough tragedy of 1989 in which 96 people were crushed to death, you'd hardly expect it to be a funky, upbeat audience-participation number.

Nicky Wire is one of British Rock's finest lyricists yet he seems to be strangely dumbstruck from the start. And during the middle and the end, come to that.

The subtext of this song, well I've thought about it for so long, they begin, before singing about how it's not the kind of thing people want to hear from The Manics. Considering this is the same Manics who covered such topics as malaria-worshipping holocaust victims, dying anorexics and self-mutilation on the four albums before this song's release in 1998, I'd argue it's exactly what people want to hear from them. And I don't think anyone would blame them for not rewriting 'Walking On Sunshine' when their guitarist is still missing, presumed dead.

They then sing, **the context of this song, well I could go on and on**, but don't even go for a single 'on', choosing instead to mutter something about principles being unfashionable.

The chorus simply concludes, **South Yorkshire Mass Murderer, how can you sleep at night?**

Good question, if we knew who the hell they were talking about. After all, even the official justice campaign for the victims hasn't ever attempted to lay the blame at the door of a single individual.

The reason for this song, well it may be a pointless one, they sing, before thanking Jimmy McGovern for writing a play about the tragedy. Yes, thanks a lot, Jimmy, you've written about it, so we don't have to. Finally, they conclude, **The ending for this song, well I haven't really thought of one**.

So let's recap. You can't tell us the subtext or context of this song (or its title, which you've inexplicably abbreviated), the reason for it is 'pointless', the chorus is vague and ultimately meaningless, and you haven't thought of an ending.

If only you hadn't thought of beginning the song in the first place.

FIVE INCREASINGLY REDUNDANT SUBJECTS FOR SONGS

4) YOUR MUM

You might have been under the impression that bad-ass gangstas, the kind who regularly claim to shoot sucker MCs in the face, have suffered from poor upbringings. On the contrary, they invariably have 'mama's who could shame Mother Theresa in terms of earthly divinity. And it's not just hip-hop artists who love their mums. Remember the Spice Girls' diabetes-inducing tribute? As yet, though, no one has yet written about their dad being bigger than your dad and having muscles bigger than He-Man and the Masters Of The Universe put together. Apart from that clap-awful 'Tractor Song'. The exception that proves the rule that rock'n'roll must always be a parent-free zone.

See: 2Pac – Dear Mama, Ghostface Killah – All That I Got Is You, Snoop Dogg – I Love My Momma

TRUE
SPANDAU BALLET

'I know this much is true,' croons Tony Hadley on this 1984 number-one hit. Yet the only truth we seem to learn from Gary Kemp's words are that he's struggling to find anything to write. After musing about being **head over heels when toe to toe**, suggesting some highly impressive contortionist skills, he tells us, **I bought a ticket to the world but now I've come back again**.

That's nice. I've just been to the toilet. But now I'm back sitting at my computer. Do carry on.

Why do I find it hard to write the next line when I want the truth to be said?

So he's come clean about his word-drought. But how to melt this particular writer's block? He mentions thrills in his head and a pill on his tongue, and even listening to 'Marvin'.

Assuming Marvin means Gaye, not Hank, then you'd have thought it might have helped. What were the working titles for this song – I Heard It In The Pipeline? Let's Get It Off? Sexual Peeling?

Either way, he gets tough with himself, and commands **Take your seaside arms and write the next line.** That first bit is from Vladimir Nabokov's *Lolita*, who is described as having 'seaside limbs and an ardent tongue'. I've got to tell you, Gaz, you'll get nowhere borrowing dirty books from your mate Sting (see Chapter 6).

Here's a better idea – why not not bother with any more words – just go 'Uh huh huh huuuuh huh' and repeat the chorus a few times? After all, writing nonsense worked for Sting too. Have you heard 'De Do Do Do De Da Da Da'?

Mmm Mmm Mmm Mmm
CRASH TEST DUMMIES

I'm sorry? What kind of title is that? 'Mmm Mmm Mmm Mmm'? Were you bound and gagged, or taking part in a cream cracker eating competition when someone asked you to give this a title?

It is, of course, the chorus of this 1993 hit. Yes, the chorus, in its entirety, goes **Mmm mmm mmm mmm**. OK, can you take that large snooker ball out of your mouth and repeat that please? **Mmm mmm mmm mmm**.

From this chasm-like imagination vacuum, we can only assume the lyricist is one of those people who just puts an 'X' when signing his name, or does his Christmas shopping in one go by buying 50 quid's worth of John Lewis vouchers. And then when he's asked if he wants sausage or bacon with his breakfast, he says, 'I'm easy'. No, mate, you're not bloody easy, you're a howling pain in the arse. Make a decision for once in your life.

That scandalous abdication of chorus-writing responsibility is all the more unfortunate given that, otherwise, this is actually quite an intriguing song, lyrically. The verses tell the story of a boy whose hair went white after a car crash, and a girl who wouldn't undress in front of people due to her birthmarks. Great potential for some insight into the human condition. And what do these Canadian cheesewits offer us to sum up this fascinating tale? **Mmm mmm mmm mmm**.

In their defence, they might argue that they're expressing the sheer impossibility of finding words to explain the vagaries of human existence.

To which I can only respond: Zzzzzzzzz . . .

School's Out
ALICE COOPER

The original classroom call to arms surely inspired a generation to go to school with their ties slightly undone, but when Alice ran out of steam halfway through, he exposed the limitations of doing away with organised education. **Well we got no class**, he sneers, **And we got no principles. We ain't got no innocence. We can't even think of a word that rhymes.**

Well, if you can't think of a word to rhyme with 'principles' then I'd argue that you'd struggle in life once school has been 'blown to pieces', and would need intensive private tuition to just gain a basic level of literacy, starting with stuff about cats sitting on mats next to postmen called Pat. Mind you, judging by some of the entries in this chapter, you'd have no trouble carving out a successful career as a songwriter.

All Apologies
NIRVANA

It's perhaps understandable that in his depressed and probably heroin-ravaged state, Kurt Cobain sometimes struggled to summon up that familiar creative magic towards the end of his career. So he ended up singing lines like **What else could I say? Everyone is gay**.

Even he should have realised that this statement, even by the provocative, extreme standards of the punk rock *oeuvre* in which he operated, wasn't going to stand up to much scrutiny.

While there's a strong argument to claim that there are considerably more homosexuals in the world than ever admit it publicly, due to the social stigma and prejudice they face, if everyone really was gay, we'd have a bit of a problem on our hands as a species.

Just imagine it. In order to keep the birth rate ticking over, we'd have to pay pairs of men and women to indulge in the distasteful business of procreating, or at the very least, develop a pretty massive artificial insemination programme.

If, on the other hand, he'd said something similarly childlike such as all girls are smelly and have fleas, we might have been able to carve out a case for him.

SOMEWHERE ELSE
RAZORLIGHT

I met a girl, recalls Johnny Borrell. Well, that's a fine start. The possibilities are pretty much endless, and we're all ears. So what happened next? **She asked me my name, I told her what it was.**

Oh come on, you can do better than that. How about *She asked me her name, I said 'names are for tombstones, baby'*? Not massively original, but an improvement. Or how about *She asked me her name, I said 'it's Rumpelstiltskin, honey, let down your hair!'* Actually, no, that's Rapunzel, isn't it? Wrong fairy tale. It's not actually that easy, this lyric writing business, is it?

CHAPTER 10

KEEPING IT REAL?

Hypocrisy, hokum and wildly unlikely claims

Public Enemy's Chuck D famously called hip-hop 'The black CNN'. And if an entire race of people are using a form of pop music as their chief source of factual information, then they're in far greater trouble than anyone ever imagined. Anyone expecting to find a reliable source of unvarnished truth in the medium of popular song is surely heading for disappointment.

Pop has always had a large streak of fantasy woven into its DNA. If we couldn't buy into the idea of acne-scarred socially dysfunctional geeks with halitosis being transformed into superhuman boy-gods the moment they stepped on a stage, we wouldn't have choked on our Findus crispy pancakes while watching *Top Of The Pops* all those years ago.

Despite that, in recent years musicians – in the rock and rap genres especially – have developed an increasing obsession with authenticity, and a desire to prove that their art is more than mere artifice, but exudes soul, social realism, and wisdom born of genuine human experience. Yet that makes them all the more likely to make statements which just don't convince when exposed to even the gentlest scrutiny. The truth is out there, but not, I'd venture, in here . . .

JENNY FROM THE BLOCK
JENNIFER LOPEZ

Two of the chief symptoms of an ego that has grown to dangerously outsized proportions are a) total lack of self-awareness and b) talking about yourself in the third person. J-Lo showed herself to be a textbook case of both on this 2002 single.

Don't be fooled by the rocks that I got, she warned, **I'm still, I'm still Jenny from the block**.

If her claims are to be believed, and she's the same now as she was back then, she must have been pretty noticeable when she was living on 'the block' with her teacher and computer programmer parents in the South Bronx.

Would there have been room for the entourage of up to 75 which she has been known to travel with? Would there be accommodation available for the specialist eyebrow assistant, and coat-carrier, both of which she reportedly employs? And how would they have felt when she demanded two rooms and several wardrobes, all to be kept at a constant temperature of 26°C, with a constant supply of fresh lilies and candles, alongside plain M&Ms and hazelnut coffee creamer?

Still, they would perhaps have tolerated it all, because, as she herself admitted, **I'm down to earth like this . . . put God first and can't forget to stay real. To me it's like breathing, yeah**.

Breathing? Surely you could get an assistant to do that for you.

Fuck Tha Police
NWA

In this stirring protest song, Ice Cube, Dre, Eazy-E and friends present themselves as defendants in a court room, putting their case against the police, who they claim are harassing them on a daily basis, without just cause.

Shining tha light in my face, and for what? asks Eazy. **Maybe it's because I kick so much butt!**

Possibly. But later in the same line, he comes up with a more convincing possibility, when he says, **or maybe cuz I blast . . . on a stupid assed nigga when I'm playin with the trigga of any Uzi or an AK.**

Yes, I would imagine that if you're randomly shooting 'niggas' with a sub-machine gun, the police would regard it as within their rights, not to mention their sworn public duty, to stop your car and shine a light in your face, and then arrest you and charge you with first-degree murder. And I've got to say, you're really not doing a great job of defending yourself here, Eazy. Or 'Eric' as your mother called you.

Herein lies the great catch-22 of Gangsta Rap lyrics. They routinely claim to be a) practising organised criminals who regularly commit murder and b) regularly stopped by the police without justification.

Now, surely the two key elements of this scenario cannot co-exist, so what are we to conclude? We know that police harassment is a genuine problem for young black men in America, so does that mean that gangsta rappers' talk of murder, pimping, dealing and larceny may be something of a fiction? Could they in fact be roughly equivalent to the compulsive liar at primary school who used to say his uncle is Murdoch from *The 'A' Team* and they have a tank in their garage (but you can't come round to see it because it's being cleaned)?

Well, I really wouldn't like to say – they might come round and 'wet' me.

FANTASY SONG TITLES TOP TEN: INSULTS

1. One Day In Your Wife
2. The First Time Ever I Saw Your Face Like A Bent Fence
3. The Only Way Is 'Up Yours'
4. Wake Me Up Before You Go F___ Yourself
5. Ain't Nothing Goin' On But You're A C***.
6. You Are The Shitstain Of My Life
7. Ooh Aah (Just A Little Bitch)
8. Have You Seen Your Mother Baby (Standing In The Shadow Offering Sexual Favours To Sailors)?
9. Don't Let Your Mum Go Down On Me
10. 22 Grand Nob

BAD COMPANY
BAD COMPANY

Just as with rappers, it's part of the job description of bar-room desperadoes to make slightly outlandish boasts about themselves, but when Paul Rodgers from these blues-rock chuggers sings, **I was born with a six-gun in my hand,** you find yourself drawing a curious mental picture of the delivery room.

'OK, Mrs Rodgers, you're doing really well, just breathe deeply, and PUSH! PUSH! . . . not long to go now . . . and PUSH, and PUSH . . . I can see the baby's head now, well done, keep pushing . . . here he comes . . . almost there now, he's . . . oh! What's that in his hand? OH MY GOD, HE'S GOT A GUN! EVERYBODY GET DOWN! CALL SECURITY! JESUS CHRIST, HOW DID THAT GET IN THERE?!'

Of course, that was the 1970s. In this security-conscious age, the mother's pistol-packing foetus would have shown up on the hospital metal detector and the baby would have been aborted by anti-terror squads before it had a chance to cause this kind of chaos.

BLAZE OF GLORY
JON BON JOVI

Rock stars are rarely contented with their lot. No sooner have they received their first platinum disc than they start reserving tickets on the first passenger flight to the moon, or launching an ill-conceived chain of fish restaurants. Jon Bon Jovi, for his sins, has always dreamed of being a cowboy, and if he can't realistically make that happen without taking a drastic pay cut to take a casual position as a ranch hand in the Nevada Desert, or inventing a time machine which would take him back to Dodge City in 1886, he can at least write songs about it. But as to exactly what kind of cowboy he is, he seems somewhat confused. On this 1990 hit from the soundtrack to the movie *Young Guns*, he tells us, **I'm a devil on the run, a six-gun lover, a candle in the wind**. A six-gun lover? You mean, you've got six penises? Do you use them one by one, or are they small enough to all fit in at once? And you're also a candle in the wind? Surely that means you're likely to get blown out long before the first 'gun' has a chance to do much damage?

He then muddies the waters further, with the assertion that **I'm a colt in your stable, I'm what Cain was to Abel, Mister Catch-me-if-you-can**.

OK, so you're a male horse of under four years old who has yet to reach the age of sexual maturity, but also someone who is prepared to kill his brother? Well, considering these factors, just how glorious a blaze are you going to go out in when your candle is finally blown out? Apart from a place in the *Guinness Book Of Records* under the 'Most Penises' category?

Lost In You
ROD STEWART

In the pursuit of seduction, many a foolish lover has written cheques which their bodies couldn't cash. But when Rod Stewart sang on this 1988 single, **I'm coming home real soon, be ready, 'cos when I do, I'm gonna make love to you like fifteen men**, he could hardly fail to disappoint.

Just how was he going to attempt this feat? Was he planning an elaborate role play, in which he would make the beast with two backs firstly as Rod Stewart, then quickly duck out of the bedroom door for a rapid costume change, returning as Stewart Rodd, a painter and decorator from Chesterfield, then reinvent himself again as Rodolfo Stewarti, a charming Italian ice cream magnate, then Rob Steward, a shy teenage shop assistant from Spennymoor, then . . . well, you get the idea. Of course, a major drawback would be that without the aid of several Viagra (which I'm confident wasn't available in 1988, even to rock aristocracy), he would struggle to maintain an erection through these many guises, and surely wouldn't be able to achieve orgasm 15 times.

Alternatively, Rod may have imagined, in his love-drunk state, that he had a worm-like ability to chop himself into pieces, each of which would live on (and presumably procreate) independently? Or less likely still, he felt sufficiently well equipped to beat Jon Bon Jovi's world record.

You Get What You Give
NEW RADICALS

On this 1999 hit Gregg Alexander took time off from writing and producing hits for the likes of Belinda Carlisle and formed The New Radicals, whose biggest hit took aim at the vacuous corporate mall-rat culture he saw in his native America, with a call to arms to 'wake up kids' and rebel against 'fakes'.

Using the unfailingly insurrectionary medium of radio-friendly soft rock, he singled out **Frenemies, who when you're down ain't your friend, Every night we smash their Mercedes-Benz**. My word, that's a serious campaign of vandalism you're talking about there, Gregg. And I'm bound to warn you that after the fourth night in a row when these frenemies' car gets smashed by this MOR studio whizz and friends, your increasingly predictable actions would almost certainly lead to your identification as the culprit, and a warrant to be issued for the arrest of Mr. G. Alexander, along with 'The Kids'.

By the end of the song he's worked himself up into a right old tizzy, and launches into a scattershot rant. **Fashion shoots with Beck and Hanson**, he spits, **Courtney Love and Marilyn Manson. You're all fakes, run to your mansions! Come around, we'll kick your ass in!**

These lines are delivered in a voice reminiscent of a child telling someone their mum smells and then running away, which does detract a little from their rhetorical force.

Further doubts have since been cast over the credibility of these threats after Marilyn Manson publicly responded to the song by saying, 'I'll crack his skull open if I see him', Alexander hastily explained that he had misunderstood the lyric, that the lines were 'nothing personal', and in fact he had only mentioned those well-known names as 'a test' to see if the media would focus on those lines rather than the serious political message (see above) that the song was imparting. He also offered Manson his Chewbacca figurine and some ice pops if he promised they could be friends again.

Either way, at the time of writing, there have been no spates of Merc-wrecking, goth-rocker ass-kickings or other teen uprisings, which suggests the song fell short of its revolutionary ambitions.

But Gregg is still fighting the good fight. Since then he has further flexed his revolutionary muscles by writing the searing anti-capitalist rant 'Life Is A Rollercoaster' for the Irish agit-pop firebrand Ronan Keating, and producing the deeply subversive Greatest Hits album for noted London anarcho-syndicalist collective S Club 7. Right on!

TAXMAN
THE BEATLES

One of the magical feats that a great pop song can sometimes achieve is to articulate the innermost concerns of the listener.

'Will you still love me tomorrow?' We've all been there.

'I will survive'? We certainly hope so.

'Harold Wilson, you bastard, you're making me pay 90 per

cent tax on some of my admittedly massive pop star earnings'? Ah, can't really say I've been in that position myself.

But that didn't stop George Harrison parodying the taxman as saying **Should five per cent appear too small, be thankful I don't take it all**.

There are few less-dignified sounds in this world than multi-millionaires moaning about their lot. And exaggerating wildly, to boot, with lines like **I'm the Taxman ... and you're working for no one but me**.

Not strictly true, George, because you're mainly 'working' for one G. Harrison, in a job that is the envy of millions and which is already well on the way to making you one of the richest musicians in history.

George mellowed with age, however, which may be one reason why we never heard him complain about the over-inflated prices fans were expected to pay for his albums, gigs and merchandise throughout his entire career. He preferred instead to moan about the inconvenient attention of fans such as the girls he sneeringly referred to as 'apple scruffs' who hung around the Beatles' studio hoping to catch a glimpse of their heroes. But then again, maybe he was right to resent them – after all, they'd been responsible for launching him into the top tax bracket in the first place.

NOBODY WEIRD LIKE ME
RED HOT CHILI PEPPERS

It has been suggested that the guitar itself is essentially designed to look like a penis extension, what with its neck protruding several feet from the crotch area in a vaguely upwards direction. And Anthony Kiedis wouldn't be the first person to suggest through the medium of song that he has extraordinary sexual prowess. But he really lets his imagination run riot on this bragathon about his own unusual predilections. **Intercourse with a porpoise is a dream for me,** he assures us. **Hell-bent on inventing a new species. Bust my britches, bless my soul!**

Well, a boy's got to have a dream, Anthony, but you may find yourself something of a disappointment to most female porpoises. Even if you do manage to make contact with these notoriously shy creatures, the ladies of the species are used to their mates having testes which swell up to a weight of 5kg or more, and I daren't even hazard a guess at the size of their penises. You may need to 'bust your britches' and develop a serious case of elephantiasis, by the looks of it, just to make sure you touch the sides when you finally get it on.

Nevertheless, Kiedis does go on to boast, **I'm a freak of nature, Walking totem pole**. Well, at least you'll be able to get 'wood'.

CHAPTER 11

IMPEACH MY BUSH

Too much information
(WARNING: PARENTAL ADVISORY – EXPLICIT LYRICS.)[1]

[1] I bet that's put you right off, hasn't it?

As we have mentioned elsewhere in this book, in certain realms of popular culture it is considered a positive practice to 'keep it real'. So forget the soaring beauty of a well-placed metaphor, and knackers to the convention of cloaking base intentions in the scanty gown of euphemism – just tell it like it is. Why waste time and energy thinking up alternative words to express fundamentally simple sentiments?

In the following examples, the artists concerned clearly felt it best to use the same words they would if they were discussing the money shots from Edward Penishands at a hardcore porn convention. You may very well wish they hadn't.

Head
PRINCE

From the very same album as the aforementioned 'Sister' (see Chapter 5), the aptly titled *Dirty Mind*, comes this touching story of our hero seducing a bride-to-be who was 'just a virgin on my way to be wed'. She impresses him with her unrivalled abilities as a fellatrix, apparently in the middle of the street, and he once more reinforces his position as the undisputed king of the single entendre, yelping, **You know you're good, girl, I think you like to go down. You wouldn't have stopped, but I came on your wedding gown**.

Ah, isn't that sweet, readers? Do you think he keeps it hanging up, unlaundered, as a permanent reminder of that first encounter? Because don't just assume that was just some one-off casual liason. There's a happy ending to this story, as they sing together.

You freak, I married you instead. Now morning, noon and night I give you head.

That's fine. Just be sure to brush your teeth afterwards.

Come
PRINCE

Prince was, of course, barely out of his teens when he wrote the lines in the previous entry, so it's perhaps understandable that he was full of exploding hormones and raging libido. By the time he released this song in 1994, he was 36, and as we can tell from these lines, considerably more sophisticated in his fantasies. **Like a splendid, open-ended celibate friend**, he purrs, **pretending Not 2 know it (come) when I blow it in your eyes**.

And not content with quite possibly hospitalising his partner by making sexual secretions into her cornea, he's got more where that, ahem, came from.

Like a strawberry, chocolate, Fender jazz, mashed potato, fuzztone (Come) all over your thighs.

Jesus, you'd need Swarfega to mop up a mixed simile like that. And still he's back for more. **Come**, he continues, **No more will U cry**. Well, as long as you keep it away from my eyes. **It's no wonder there's a puddle there, holding it in 4 so long**.

Stop right there! Do the mashed potato fuzztone where you like, but we draw the line at water sports. Pervert.

I WANNA SEX YOU UP
COLOR ME BADD

There's nothing like a bit of fantasy and dirty talk to spice up your love life (it says here, in Deidre's photo casebook in *The Sun*), but these short-lived US soulsters took it to another level (and we're not talking about the boy band) when they purred, **Girl, you make me feel real good, we can do it til we both wake up**. You've heard of sleep talking, and even sleep walking, but sleep-shagging? Crivens, is there a Channel 5 producer in the house? The title of the documentary's there already – 'The Couple Who Have Sex In Their Sleep'. A BAFTA nomination is surely a mere formality.

I suppose it's fair enough for lone individuals to enjoy themselves sexually while in the land of nod – if only my parents didn't keep turning up uninvited during my regular dream-trysts with Miranda Richardson, I might actually achieve orgasm – but for two people to indulge in sexual activity together only stopping when they wake up – well this is the stuff of science fiction. Sci-fi porn in fact – a relatively neglected genre since *Flesh Gordon*[1].

Their imaginations stretch further than that too. Later in the song they vow to **make love until we drown**. Oh, honestly, now you're just being silly . . .

---

[1] A 70s soft-porn spoof on *Flash Gordon* (well, you probably guessed it wasn't Dan Dare) which, urban myth has it, was occasionally hired accidentally for children's parties by unsuspecting parents. I can confirm, however, that it was most often hired by teenage boys who persuaded someone's older brother to take their parents' video card to the shop and hire it for them, whereupon they were deeply underwhelmed to find that it was about as erotic as a Benny Hill sketch. Starring Bob Todd[2].
[2] Diminutive bald man who spent a large proportion of his working life being kissed on the head and then slapped in the face by women. It's a living, I suppose.

Indian Girl (An Adult Story)
SLICK RICK

The problem of sexually transmitted infections has been poorly served in pop lyrics, possibly because this is a form of music that is generally meant to encourage you to have sex, not put you off it for life. So we should perhaps respect the pioneering spirit of this hip-hop hard man's 1988 tale, in which our hero consummates a casual 'relationship' with a Native American woman, only to get a nasty surprise when he ventures 'down south'. **He wanted to see the vagina face to face**, he explains. **He opened it up, with his bare two thumbs. He seen crabs with SPEARS AND INDIAN DRUMS! They's going heya hiya heya hey, hey**!

Are you sure this was the result of VD and not a really scary acid trip, Rick? It's just that, unless she was actually dead, and there was some sort of grotesque infestation of her corpse, the spears and Indian drums side of things would surely defy scientific explanation. And besides, crabs are generally found in the infected individual's pubic h— . . . OK, I think we'll move on now.

Flower
LIZ PHAIR

Voices of unfettered female lust have been heard very rarely in comparison to their rutting, leery male counterparts, but it's comforting to know that when they do make their most base feelings known, they sound every bit as daft.

This memorable outburst from the US singer-songwriter's acclaimed 1993 debut album was highly refreshing in its refusal to cloak its meaning in gentle metaphors and oblique innuendo.

I want to fuck you like a dog, she growled, **I'll take you home and make you like it**.

Surely you can't have it both ways, Liz. If you want to simulate a typical canine sexual encounter then surely I, the male partner, will have to mount you from behind, then kind of walk around a little while hanging out of the back of you, and achieve orgasm within a couple of seconds, before wandering off and sniffing another woman's bottom. Is that really your idea of the ultimate lovemaking experience?

She's not in the mood to listen to reason though. She continues in the same horny vein, admitting, **I just want your fresh young jimmy, jamming, slamming, ramming in me,** finally concluding, **Everything you ever thought of is everything I'll do to you, I'll fuck you 'til your dick is blue**.

That might take some time. And I would imagine we'd have to travel to a very cold environment in order to achieve the requisite hue of my appendage. By which time it would surely be in the first stages of frostbite, and eventually drop off, which would be no good to man or bitch.

All things considered, then, shall we just go for a drink and see how we get on?

FIVE REALLY ANNOYING THINGS LYRICISTS DO

1) SING 'SINGING . . . '

It's the songwriter's equivalent of coasting to the finish line
– sitting back in the saddle, hands free to acknowledge the
acclaim of the crowd, and encouraging them to sing with you
all the way home, 'Singing . . . '

Except half the time they're about to stop singing, and just
make a series of sounds with their mouth. In fact, often they
follow it with something most fans would feel deeply
embarrassed to utter if there weren't 15,000 other droogs
around who would gladly light their own farts if their glorious
leader commanded it.

As Chris Martin wrote on 'X&Y', 'You and me are floating on
a tidal wave together, you and me are drifting into outer
space, singing . . . OOOOOOOOOH OOOOOOH'

If I was Gwynnie, I'd be saying, 'Sorry, Chris, I'm enjoying
our ride on a tidal wave just as much as you, especially now
we're inexplicably drifting into the stratosphere, and I would
do anything for love, but . . . I won't sing that. What if someone
films me and it ends up on Youtube?'

2) STAND IN THE RAIN

'Why does it always rain on me?' Because it's your job as a
songwriter to spend a disproportionate amount of your time
there. You'll invariably be standing in it, usually having been
'left' there by a romantic partner.

It's always a suitable place to be dumped because so many significant romantic scenes in Hollywood romantic comedies coincide with unexpected rainstorms of monsoon proportions, whether they're breaking up, begging forgiveness or finally indulging in that long-awaited tongue sandwich (which they continue with regardless of the inclement weather, because they're THAT into each other).

You might well ask why someone can't, just for a change, break up or make up in blazing sunshine. But like a locust wiggling its antennae in China, that could upset the delicate balance of the universe. It's the law – now get out there and soak it up.

3) SWEAR THAT 'WE'LL MAKE IT'

Make it to where? The promised land? To the church on time? To the pub before last orders?

Or are they talking about making something, in reference to their plan to bake a cake, or build a wendy house, or make a plasticine dog, while secretly harbouring romantic desires for their construction partner?

Either way, just saying 'we'll make it' is too vague for anyone's comfort. You're not going to reassure an insecure partner by saying 'we'll make it' – it sounds like you're being elusive, like replying to the words 'I love you' with the words 'That's nice, dear'.

4) WRITE ABOUT NOT BEING ABLE TO WRITE ANY WORDS

If this was a game show, you'd be able to pass, or play your joker, but unfortunately you have to write something – so why not write about the frustrations of not being able to write? You can always fudge it, and outline some opaque guff about being tongue-tied, which could apply to a relationship but which are really about the bottomless black hole where your creative inspiration should be.

Why, if you really want to take the piss, you can even call it 'Untitled'.

5) END THE SONG WITH THE WORD 'END'

Just like the person who drops a coin in the newsagent and quips, 'Oops! I'm throwing it away! Ha ha!', songwriters still think it's clever to end a song with that very word.

They think it sounds as if they're announcing 'The End', as if this were an old movie or something. It helps them maintain the delusion that they're telling a story, rather than stringing together a bunch of tangentially linked musings about writer's block. Not remotely big, or clever, I would cont . . . end.

WORK IT
MISSY ELLIOT

Understandably tired of the fellas having all the fun with their bawdy locker-room bravado, hip-hop has seen a number of female artists take the same uncensored lyrical approach to sexual relations. Some will, of course, find this a vital blow for female empowerment. And some . . . well, consider this come-hither spiel: **Call before you come, I need to shave my cho-cha, You do or you don't or you will or won't cha, Go downtown and eat it like a vulture.**

That's a tempting offer, Missy. But I'm disturbed by that last demand. How exactly should I eat it like a vulture? Is your 'cho-cha' actually dead? If the process of putrefaction is setting in then I imagine it might not be too tasty.

Besides, this whole proposition is getting stranger by the minute. Shortly afterwards, she promises, **Take my thong off and my ass go boom!**

I'd rather not get too close when that happens.

THONG SONG
SISQO

As a single gentleman, you would surely be ill-advised to copy the seduction tactics and smooth talking of your favourite pop performers, if you don't want to remain single forever.

For instance, let us consider the following appraisal of a

young lady: **She had dumps like a truck truck truck, Thighs like what what what. Baby move your butt butt butt**.

So how would that play out in a typical nightclub situation? Leaning closer to your chosen quarry on the dancefloor, you beckon her towards you, and loosen your silver tongue: 'I'd just like to say, Miss, that you have dumps like a truck.'

If you survived without suffering physical violence, then you could perhaps move on to the next stage of your amorous onslaught. 'And those thighs! They're like ... what?'

She still there? She's just playing hard to get. Move in for the kill, soldier!

'Baby, move your butt, butt butt.'

She'd surely get the message at this point, and proceed to vacate the area with indecent haste.

TWO GUYS FOR EVERY GIRL
PEACHES

We could fill this whole chapter with the musings of this Canadian electro-vamp, author of songs such as 'Fuck The Pain Away' and 'Slippery Dick', and the woman who would surely have won our 'album title of 2003' award, had there been one, with her collection *Fatherfucker*. She particularly excelled herself on this paean to threesomes from her 2006 album *Impeach My Bush*. It suggested that boys should get it on with each other while she watches, before inviting her to join the fun.

Somehow, I doubt this idea will catch on in quite the same way as the two-girls-one-boy scenario that has now become a staple of mainstream porn, but the broad-minded among you will surely admire her sense of adventure. **I wanna see you boys get down with each other, I wanna see you do your 'lil 'nasty brother**, she pants. OK, there's nothing wrong with voicing your innermost fantasies. But hang on, what's this? **I'll slink in when you boys are in a French knot, we play a game it's like your gonna get caught, that's the time you're gonna get so damn hot, you wanna see my pussy pop pop pop**.

Sounds tempting. But let's just iron out a few technicalities before we dive in here, though. 'French knot'? Isn't that some kind of sewing technique? That sounds painful. And what exactly is your 'pussy' going to do again? Are you advocating the use of fireworks? Any chance of getting my willy insured before I go anywhere near you? Or him?

FIVE INCREASINGLY REDUNDANT SUBJECTS FOR SONGS

5) DRUGS ARE GREAT / OH NO, ACTUALLY DRUGS ARE TERRIBLE AND YOU SHOULDN'T DO THEM, EVEN THOUGH I HAVE AND HAD A BLOODY BRILLIANT TIME

If I went home after five pints of Carling Extra Cold and wrote a song about how great Carling Extra Cold was as its cool crisp-tasting liquid soothed the fire in my ever-expanding belly, I'd be rightly dismissed as a dribbling pub rock bore with stale lager where my brain cells should be. But five pints of cocaine? Or heroin? Feel free to impart thy wisdom from your travels down the road of excess! We won't even question the fact that you can't consume heroin in pints.

And when you've milked that subject into a shrivelled old teat and finally kicked the habit, why not write some more songs comparing your drug addiction to a demonic possession, and then in interviews, tell us why we shouldn't do what you've spent the last five albums glamorising.

Thankfully, unlike you, we're not arrogant, stupid or rich enough to think that a drug habit would be a good idea, but don't let that stop you patronising us with the kind of stuff we learned shortly after leaving primary school.

See also: Red Hot Chili Peppers – 'Under The Bridge' / 'Snow (Hey Oh)'; Oasis – 'Morning Glory' / 'Gas Panic'; Primal Scream – 'Higher Than The Sun' / 'Exterminator'

FANTASY SONG TITLE TOP TEN:
FETISH

1. MAD ABOUT THE VOYEUR
2. MASTERS OF WATER SPORTS
3. CAN'T TAKE MY EYES OFF SHOES
4. MUSIC TO WATCH GIRLS' THIGHS
5. HAVE I TOLD YOU LATEX THAT I LOVE YOU?
6. FROTTEUR WONDERFUL WORLD
7. RUBBER MAN, OH WHERE CAN YOU BE?
8. I WOULD DO ANYTHING FOR SUB-DOM (BUT I WON'T DO THAT)
9. UPTOWN TOP SPANKIN'
10. GOD'S COPROPHILIA

FIGURE YOU OUT
NICKELBACK

There should be no limits to the outrageous things that people say to each other in the privacy of their own bedroom. The problem comes when they start sharing them with millions, as if they were Peter Stringfellow doing the hustle with Kerry Katona on a podium in the middle of Trafalgar Square. It's at that point where we have to draw the line.

I love your pants around your feet, pants Chad Kroeger on this deeply distasteful outburst, **and I love the dirt that's on**

your knees. OK, so she's playing the role of some downtrodden Dickensian scullery maid – she must be thrilled! **I like the way you still say please while you're looking up at me**, he grunts. Are you paying her for this? **You're like my favourite damn disease**. Well, let's hope it's life-threatening, you horrible, horrible man.

LITTLE THINGS
BUSH

Maybe we should cut some slack for the slavering pervs in this chapter. After all, when overcome with unclean thoughts, it's only natural to abandon normal considerations of decorum and decency and make a massive twerp of yourself, like drunken sales reps cavorting in the middle rows of Emirates economy class. But when it comes to songwriting, you would normally have a chance to take another look at the gurning crap you wrote while squinting with lust, and realise your hard-won artistic reputation could be at risk if such words make it into recorded form. Luckily, Bush had little reputation to lose when Gavin Rossdale sang, **I touch your mouth, My willy is food**. I'm presuming that if he was involved in any internet-based cannibal sex ring it would have been in the news by now, so surely he's sending out the wrong message to any of the more impressionable groupies out there. Maybe a sequel to this song, along the lines of NWA's 'Just Don't Bite It', would be wise in case anyone gets the wrong idea.

CHAPTER 12

CAREER RHYMINALS

*For those who continue to suck . . .
we salute you!*

To produce one bad rhyme in a career may be regarded as misfortune. To produce three or four might be regarded as carelessness, or worse still, the kind of creative bankruptcy that provokes people to lazily rewrite famous Oscar Wilde quotes. Consider the following repeat offenders.

LOVE
ARTHUR LEE

Arthur Lee of Love took full advantage of the psychedelic era's creative licence when he wrote the words to their classic album *Forever Changes*. On 'The Red Telephone', for instance, he muses, **I believe in Magic. Why? Because it is so quick**. Little did he know that David Blaine would one day take three months to do a single stunt. However, it sounds like the only magic that could possibly have been at work in this song were the mushroom variety, considering he then sang **... I feel real phoney when my name is Bill ... or was that Phil?**

Elsewhere on that same album, on 'Live And Let Live' he sings, **Oh the snot has caked against my pants, it has turned into crystal. There's a bluebird sitting on a fence, I think I'll take my pistol. I've got it in my hand, because he's on my land**.

Now, you might want to sit down and pour yourself a stiff drink before I break this to you, but Arthur Lee later admitted to being somewhat stoned when he penned those lines. Say it ain't so!

T-REX
MARC BOLAN

Clearly affected by a similar variety of 'magic', the would-be glam idol was evidently operating on a higher spiritual plane during his time as part of Tyrannosaurus Rex. On the title track of the album *She Was Born To Be My Unicorn* he wrote, **The night-mare's mauve mashed mind, sights the visions of the blinds. Shoreside stream of steam. Cooking kings in cream of scream**.

It's comforting to know that if Bolan hadn't made it in the music business, he could have enjoyed a lucrative career writing tongue twisters for joke books.

He'd come back to earth somewhat by 1971, though, when on 'Cosmic Dancer' he asked rhetorically, **What's it like to be a loon? I liken it to a balloon**. Yet he was. He was still playing fast and loose with conventional meaning when on Woodland Rock he noted, **Met a little Momma, she was sweet, she was gone. She's got legs like a railroad, Face like a song**. Luckily, he was already well on the way to inventing glam rock, in which verbal eloquence was not the primary concern, hence him getting away with lines like **She's my woman of gold and she's not very old** ('Hot Love'), or **I drive a Rolls Royce, it's good for my voice** ('Children Of The Revolution').

NEW ORDER
BERNARD SUMNER

This man has been caning couplets for decades now, and he's not always fussy as to the quality when he's keen for his next fix. On 'Slow Jam', for instance, he noted **The sea was very rough, It made me feel sick. But I like that kind of stuff, it beats arithmetic**.

A thought that will strike a chord with anyone who has been

faced with the daily dilemma of whether to throw up or do some sums.

On 'Every Second Counts', he sang, **every second counts when I am with you. I think you are a pig, you should be in a zoo.** But if that leads you to think our hero lacks a romantic streak, you are so wrong. In fact Sumner is at his most enigmatic on the eternally unfathomable subject of love. Consider 'Crystal', on which he notes, **here comes love, it's like honey, you can't buy it with money.** I suppose love is a bit like honey – you know, kind of sweet, can be sticky if you do it without protection, but on the other hand, it's also like a colour, as Bernard observed on 'Guilt Is A Useless Emotion', with the lines **real love can't be sold, it's another colour than gold.** Well that narrows it down on the colour front – could it be dark plum, or burnt russet? Pale cream? Flaccid yellow? All rather confusing, but thankfully, on 'Sub-Culture' he offers a more basic appraisal of relationships, with the warning, **One of these days when you sit by yourself, you'll realise you can't shaft without someone else.** Can't really argue with that.

SUEDE
BRETT ANDERSON

A chronic rhyming habit has been noted in other eminent recording artists, not least this Britpop alumnus. Around the time of Suede's third album, *Coming Up*, their lyricist seemed to develop an alarming predilection for winceworthy lines, not least the one on 'She' in which he spoke of **She, shaking up the karma, She, injecting mari-joo-ana**. You had to ask what exactly a self-confessed chemical gourmand like Anderson could possibly be thinking of. We could perhaps forgive the likes of St Winifred's School Choir for being a touch sketchy on the finer details of recreational cannabis use, but he must know only too well that injecting marijuana is nigh on impossible. And as for its pronunciation, is he trying to play dumb in case the drug squad are listening? There's no point playing the innocent, Brett, they've heard those other songs, and lines like 'let's chase the dragon', 'I'm aching to see my heroine' and 'All I want for christmas is a crack sandwich'. The game's up, son.

Soon after, on 'Savoir Faire', he wrote, **She lives in a house, she's stupid as a mouse**. However, despite this modest appraisal, he noted, **she's got savoir faire, yeah yeah**. Sounds like one hell of a lady! Her own accommodation, almost completely unintelligent, but nevertheless has some sort of basic 'know-how' which presumably means she'll be quite practical when it comes to cooking, cleaning, that kind of thing. Why, you've got yourself quite a catch there, Brett!

She must have been particularly tolerant of his eccentric ways, however, judging by the lines on 'Head Music' when he yelps, **Give me head, give me head, give me head music instead**.

Make your mind up, lover boy! One minute you're desperate for some intimate oral attention, and then when she's just reaching for the zipper, you tell her 'Actually, on second thoughts, I'd rather put some Brian Eno on'. That's got to be tough for any woman to swallow. Metaphorically speaking.

KAISER CHIEFS
RICKY WILSON

Most of the above lyrics may seem a little less than contemporary, coming, as they do, from the last century. So it's good to know there are plenty of artists still out there who are prepared to play fast and loose with poetic convention, and marry words together in the songwriter's equivalent of a shotgun marriage. This Leeds quintet dragged fingernails down imaginary blackboards in 2003 when their breakout hit 'I Predict A Riot' began with the lines **Watching The People Get Lairy, It's Not Very Pretty I Tell Thee**. You will also have noticed their coupling of 'name tag on it' and 'plate tectonic' on 'Oh My God', as discussed in more depth in Chapter 2.

But since then they've raised the bollocks bar to ambitious new heights, as we witness on their 2007 number 'Saturday Night'. Consider the passage:

Pneumothorax is a word that is long, They're just trying to put some punk back into punctured lung.

Panic over, party off, party on, 'cos we are birds of a feather and you can be the fat one.

In a recent interview, they admitted that lyric writing is a collaborative process for them. Which surely confirms the ancient wisdom which defines a camel as 'a horse, designed by committee'.

U2
BONO

You can sometimes excuse the young and naive of their momentary descents into schoolboy doggerel in the early days of their careers. When U2 were first signed, Bono had still yet to perfect his stock in trade of writing vague impressionistic rhetoric about rivers running dry in the desert of the American night. On their early song 'Trevor', U2 informed us **Trevor seems quite clever, but Trevor lives forever. Trevor is together, Trevor whatever**. Innocent enough, really, but if rhyme is, as we suggested, like a drug, U2 were clearly getting dabbling in the hallucinogenic variety by the time they released 'Some Days Are Better Than Others' on their *Zooropa* album in 1993. **Some days are dry, some days are leaky,** he sings, **some days come clean, other days are sneaky. Some days take less but most days take more, they slip through your fingers and onto the floor.**

I know what he means. What a week I've had. A leaky Monday, a sneaky Tuesday, then I spent all day Thursday cleaning Wednesday off the floor. Mind you, it's nothing compared to last winter. Next door had a pipe full of 23rd February burst on them, and it flooded the whole of March.

Anyway, Bono dabbled relatively sparingly in such sentence-altering substances until 2000, when he fell off the wagon big time on 'Elevation'. **Got no self-control,** he admitted, not before time, **been living like a mole now, going down, excavation. High and high in the sky, you make me feel like I can fly, So high, elevation.**

I think you're having another leaky day, Bono. How about a nice lie down?

Bob Dylan

As we have seen elsewhere in this volume, the spokesman for a generation trod in a few cowpats on the rocky road to greatness, even in his peerless mid-60s prime. It's hard to forget the line from 'I Want You' when he sings, **Now your dancing child with his Chinese suit, he spoke to me, I took his flute. No, I wasn't very cute . . . to him, was I?**

A serious motorcycle accident didn't really do much to knock any sense into him, and on 'Lo And Behold', recorded in 1967 but released on *The Basement Tapes* in 1975, he sang, **What's the matter Molly dear, what's the matter with your mound? What's it to ya Moby Dick, this is chicken town!**

That's right, Bob.

Thankfully, by the mid-1970s he seemed keen that the odd listener should actually understand what he had to say, and the epic protest song 'Hurricane' exemplifies this new approach. Yet despite such lucidity, he performed a trick beloved of rhyminals everywhere – shoving a square peg in a round hole, with the line **We're gonna put his ass in stir / We're going to pin this triple mur . . . der on him, he ain't no gentleman Jim!**

Here we see a word that straddles two lines as comfortably as an athlete landing crotch-first on a hurdle. It hurts even to watch it. Still, this is the man who later wrote…wait for it…'Wiggle wiggle wiggle, Like a bowl of soup', so he clearly has a high pain threshold.

Eric B & Rakim
Rakim

Awarded almost regal status within the hip-hop 'game', the rapping half of pioneering 80s duo has been praised in rarified literary circles (well, *The Source* magazine, maybe) for his pioneering use of internal rhyming (writing rhymes within the same lines – there, that's street knowledge if you care to share), but it's a dangerous path to tread. Especially when, on 'Paid In Full', he mentions some of the things he enjoys in his spare time. He lists a **tape of Me and Eric B, and a nice big plate of fish, which is my favorite dish. But without no money it's still a wish**.

Of course, once their debut album went platinum, they were wealthy enough to listen to tapes of themselves and stuff themselves *full,* of cod, haddock and *macker-ull*. I dare say they had them stacked on *shelves*, to suit *themselves*, or were even served them by *elves* so they didn't have to *delve*, and get their fingers all sticky.

You can't buy a poetic licence, and Rakim came close to having it revoked on 'Follow The Leader', when he exhorted, **Dance! Cuts rip your pants! Eric B. on the blades, bleedin' death, call an ambulance!**

Even if we disregard the rhyme of 'pants' with 'ambulance', it's a good job such injury-inducing music isn't being made in the more litigious 21st century, or there would surely be TV adverts, featuring a badly acted reconstruction of a man's pants being ripped by the sheer force of the DJ's 'cuts', and then the question: 'Have you been a victim of an accident in a nightclub which wasn't your fault? Possibly involving cuts which rip your pants? Well call "Hip-hop Injury Lawyers" today. Don't delay, it's the only way. Word to the mother, HHIL – there ain't no other.' They'd surely have a watertight case, and would leave our deadly duo skint and fish-free once more.

You might regard such flinch-inducing lines as fundamentally harmless. But there were evidently young impressionable rappers out there copying them. Assuming you're reading this book chronologically, rather than dipping into the odd bit while waiting for the turtle's head, then you will have seen the entry about Snap's 'Rhythm Is A Dancer' in Chapter 1. Bearing that in mind does the following passage ring any bells? **'I got a question, serious as cancer – who can keep the the average dancer, hyper as a heart attack, nobody smilin'?'.**

Elsewhere, on 'Microphone Fiend', Rakim bragged, **back to the problem, I got a habit. You can't solve it, silly rabbit!** The same ridiculous phrase was later used by Public Enemy, who wrote in 'Don't Believe The Hype', **I see the tape recorder and I grab it. No you can't have it back, silly rabbit!**

Que? It turns out that the phrase comes from a US advert for breakfast cereal, in which a rabbit tries to steal the cereal and is told, 'Silly rabbit! Trix are for kids!'

It all makes perfect sense now.

CHAPTER 13

THE BOTTOM 10

The worst song lyrics in the world . . . ever!

It had to happen. Just as surely as 'alright' follows 'Saturday night', I was destined to sum up this book by picking a list of my worst ever lyrics. While I would love to arrange a phone poll for which all you gullible rubes would ring a premium-rate line 50 times in a day just to ensure that 'Rhythm Is A Dancer' grabs the top spot, I am just doing this out of the sourness of my own heart. And to get a bit of publicity for the book from whining Bob Dylan fans who want to burn me at the stake for dissing Rock's own poet laureate.

I made a half-arsed attempt at making this scientific by working out how many different kinds of lyrical crime these songs could be accused of, and adding them in brackets, but then I've mostly ignored that and just put it in whichever order I feel like. To give this an element of surprise I'll announce my findings in reverse order, notwithstanding the fact that you'll only have to glance at the opposite page to find out what's number one.

10. SNAP – 'RHYTHM IS A DANCER'

[Bad rhyming, inappropriate sentiments, nonsense, illogical, uninspired]

A link between cancer and dancing is suggested with the kind of crude insensitivity that even *The Daily Mail* would baulk at. I won't say any more – or he will attack, and we don't want that.

9. THE CRYSTALS – 'HE HIT ME AND IT FELT LIKE A KISS'

[inappropriate sentiments, illogical]

Avoids a bottom-five finish due to the singularity of its offence, but nonetheless, this is a lyric jaw-dropping enough to make any self-respecting female throw themselves in front of a racehorse in protest.

8. BILLY JOEL – 'WE DIDN'T START THE FIRE'

[bad rhymes, inappropriate sentiments, well meaning but still rubbish]

Imagine world events reduced to the equivalent of the conveyor belt memory test on *The Generation Game*. While it was comforting to know that Billy Joel was not responsible for the invention of the Hydrogen bomb or the Belgian intervention in the Congo, he perhaps bit off more than he could chew by trying to cover half a century in the space of five minutes. And he forgot the fondue set and cuddly toy.

7. DEF LEPPARD – 'POUR SOME SUGAR ON ME'

(innuendo, bad rhymes, nonsense)

Food sex with Def Leppard anyone? You've got the peaches, they've got the cream. And the courts have got a restraining order ready to go, just press that panic button if they come within 200 yards.

6. RICHARD HARRIS/DONNA SUMMER 'MACARTHUR PARK'

(bad rhymes, illogical, nonsense, obscure)

Another lyric which fell spectacularly off the surrealist tightrope. It does, however, retain a certain kitsch charm, unlike most other songs in this list. Why, who hasn't felt themselves 'pressed in love's hot, fevered iron like a striped pair of pants' from time to time?

5. BOB DYLAN – 'BALLAD OF A THIN MAN'

(bad rhymes, obscure, nonsense, illogical)

'Don't criticise what you can't understand' he once said. So that means no one on planet earth has the right to have a pop at this rampant tosh – Idi Amin couldn't have justified it better, Bob. But traditionalist as this view may be, I do hold that no good can come from writing a lyric that reads like *The Times* cryptic crossword.

A throat-borrowing sword swallower in high heels, contacts with the lumberjacks, a 'cow'-shouting one-eyed midget and tax deductible charity organisations – what can it all mean? Could the Dylan who wrote this song be a surrealist relative of Chauncey Gardiner from The Peter Sellers film *Being There*? Full of mysterious statements which no-one, least of all Mr Jones, understands, but wishfully imbues with great significance? Or is he just having a laugh at our expense?

4. THE CRANBERRIES – 'I JUST SHOT JOHN LENNON'

(bad rhymes, nonsense, illogical, well-meaning but still rubbish)

A song about the death of an icon by the woman who gave us 'Zombie' and 'Bosnia was so unkind'? We had instinctively known it wouldn't be nice.

You've heard of the tribute song, now welcome to the insult song. An impossibly clumsy Irish jig on the great man's grave.

3. AMERICA – 'HORSE WITH NO NAME'

(bad rhymes, illogical, uninspired, obscure)

Heat that was 'hot' but only produced mild suntans, anonymous equines with supernatural endurance, plants and rocks and things, and oceans like deserts. A horse with no name, and a song making no sense. Avoids the number one spot due to a jolly nice tune.

2. STEVE MILLER BAND – 'THE JOKER'

(bad rhymes, innuendo, bullshit, nonsense, inappropriate sentiments)

A quick trawl of the world wide web reveals Mr Miller took most of the toe-gnawing phrases from this song from his own previous compositions. That's right, Space cowboy, Gangster of love, 'Maureeeece' (cue guitar wolf-whistle that makes you want to bite down on a grenade) – he's so proud of them he sampled himself. Then he made up the word 'pompatus of love' just to throw some repetition and farcical gibberish into the mix. Then even when he nicked the peaches, tree shaking, and lovey dovey from an old doo-wop song, he sounded as seductive as a fat tramp pleasuring himself in a bush. Truly foul.

1. BLACK EYED PEAS – 'MY HUMPS'

(bad rhymes, innuendo, bullshit, nonsense, inappropriate sentiments)

A teacher friend of mine recently invited a class of 11-year-olds to invent a dance to a song of their choice, which they would perform in front of the school. They chose this funky little number, and proceeded to bump, grind, grab their nonexistent 'humps' and generally make an entire school feel like swallowing itself with embarrassment. As for the rest of us, well, we still can't even look at cocoa puffs without shuddering in disgust. Shame on a nuclear scale.

CHAPTER 14

THE PERFECT STORM

I don't find it hard to write the next line

One of the main complaints made by musicians whose work is criticised by sneering smartarses like me is that we could never actually write songs ourselves. Well, I beg to differ. Not only can I write a song (albeit not very well), but I'm sure I can write a lyric even worse than anything in this book.

I put myself in the position of a harassed songwriter and tried to encompass most of the major lyrical crimes within my composition. I'm not one to boast, but I'd like to think of this as something of a perfect storm of bad lyrics. Read 'em and weep . . .

UNTITLED

(c. J. Sharp, 2009.)[1]

I wrote a song for you . . . and it goes a little something like this . . .

I saw you standing in the rain
Feeling the agony of pain
Looked like you wished you were in Spain
I said excuse me, you look like you need a little company
You smiled through the tears and you said 'my boyfriend's
dumped me'

I sat down beside you and I held your hand
you said hey, you look like you should be in a band
We talked of movies, films and books
And our favourite bits from Spooks
I thought as sure as a great author . . . was Nabokov
Well tonight I'm going to get your . . . knickers off
I can see that my buzz makes your honey drip,
bzzz, bzzz come on put this sting between your lips

CHORUS:
Cos I can't find the words that'll say
How much I wanna have my way . . . with you
And your twin sister too
Girl I think you want it too— hoo hoo,
Or am I totally delu-hoo-hoo . . . ded?

Then she saw my love starting to grow
She said I'd rather take it slow
Let's just go and have a drink
But I could see she was turning pink
I said sorry to be blunt but I really thought it worth a punt
I don't want you to think of me as a cheeky runt
You see its not that I have no respect for you it's
Just I can't stop looking at your RAF targets

CHORUS:

All the great poets have tried to sum it up
And all I can say is I'd like to drink your furry cup
Lorca spoke of love in solitude
100 years of gonorrheas couldn't kill my love for you
And when I finally recovered
I just know we'd still be lovers
And so she came in from the rain
And I said I'll see you again . . . some time

Singing la la la la la lain
Ta ta ta ta ta ta train
Come on come on sing it again
Singing la la la la lain
(Right until the end)

[1] *Just in case you were thinking of nicking it and having a worldwide number one hit with it)*

ACKNOWLEDGEMENTS

For every book that comes out, there are many scores of people without whom it could never have happened. Or so you'd imagine from reading their acknowledgement pages. In truth, of course, if half of them had been wiped out by a flesh-eating virus, the books might still have come out, but it would have been very inconvenient for all concerned. So I'll acknowledge the people who have helped me with this book by saying this book might not have been thought of if it wasn't for me, and my possession of a fully functioning brain and an interest in popular music. It might not have been hawked round various publishers with such determination without the hard work of my agent Susan Smith. Some of the worst offenders might have escaped undetected without the nominations of everyone who suggested their own favourite crap lyrics on obscure internet message boards so they would come up on my google searches. I can't thank you enough – even the ones who put 'LOL' after they mentioned them.

This book would almost certainly not have come out without the enthusiasm and advice of Tom Bromley, late of Portico Books, and also would have withered on the vine without similar attributes on the part of his successor Malcolm Croft. I would like to apologise to both for my unkind words regarding Bob Dylan. Then again, no – the whiney cryptic curmudgeon deserves all he gets.

I'd also like to thank my friends for their helpful suggestions, and apologise for all the times I steered perfectly serviceable conversations unwillingly back to the topic of crap lyrics.

Finally, I'd like to apologise to my mum for any swearing. I don't think there is much, unless you count that nasty Paul Weller in Chapter 8, but as you always maintained, it just shows he's got nothing more intelligent to say.